For all the attendees of the presentation that served as a seed for this book. Especially those who told me it helped you. I wouldn't have believed this was useful without you.

Structuring Life to Support Creativity

A Resource Book for Creative People

Sandra Tayler

Hypernode Press

Hypernode Press
an imprint of the Tayler Corporation

Print on Demand 2nd Edition

Cover art & design by Melissa Williams Design
Layout by Sandra Tayler
Editing by A.J. Jepperson, Bob Defendi, and Linda Newville

Galley review by Hayley Hess-Beaumont, Heidi Darley,
Daphne Higbee, Melissa Muhlenkamp, and Wendy Morkel

Copy editing by Beth Anderson

No generative AI was used in the creation of this book.

Printed on Demand location variable
10 9 8 7 6 5 4 3 2

Contents

Introduction

Welcome!

As you enter, I want to give you a quick orientation on what this book has to offer you.

You opened these pages with a question in mind, a curiosity you hope I will answer. I join you in that hope. I'll present lots of ideas, solutions, and activities for you to explore. This book is like a show home in a new development: set up to display customizable options for you to begin to picture what might work in your life. Some of what's on display will not suit you. I invite you to pass those options by and only select the ones that make your life better. Also, unlike most home tours, here you're invited to poke into odd corners and examine the pipes under the sink. I want you to understand how this house works, which will serve you far better than admiring light fixtures and fancy countertops.

For your tour, I've organized the sections of this book into a deliberate flow of information. Within each section are chapters containing stories and concepts along with activities to help you find the best ways to apply those concepts in your life. Some activities build on each other, others are alternate approaches to the same challenge. Looking at challenges from multiple angles can be helpful in finding an insight or solution. Feel free to opt out of any activity that doesn't help you or feels repetitive. The lists you make as part of activities are temporary exercises to be changed or discarded when they're no longer useful. Making a list helps you absorb information and does not require you to abide by that list in the future. The activities lean toward self-introspection and writing (my natural modes), but you should do the activities in whatever way best helps you. People process information differently. Some process better by conversing with a friend rather than by writing a list. Others need to make collages or create visual arrangements of the information. Just like in a new home, feel free to add embellishments or paint to any idea you like. It is your house. Yours to change as you wish.

If you are willing to put yourself into my hands and read the chapters in order, I will carry you from concept to concept, each one introducing and supporting the next. Together they create a structure, which is what this book is about.

As your host, I may mention upcoming ideas. If your heart says "Oooh! I want that now," feel free to jump ahead to that new thought. You can always come back and read the others later. After all, you came to this book with a question. If you see the answer to your question, why not satisfy that need first, then return later to absorb the rest?

In fact, let's make this your first activity a choose your own adventure of sorts.

Preview Activity
See What Is Offered

Purpose: To give you a sense of what information is coming and allow you to find urgent solutions before settling in to read.

Flip through this book or scan the table of contents to see if a particular chapter calls to you. Spot read a paragraph, or an entire chapter. If an activity feels relevant and useful, go ahead and try it.

Then return here and let me take you on the rest of this tour. There are hidden treasures in this house that you won't know you need until you examine them.

Thank you for joining me. I have much to show you. Let's get started.

Creativity and Dreams

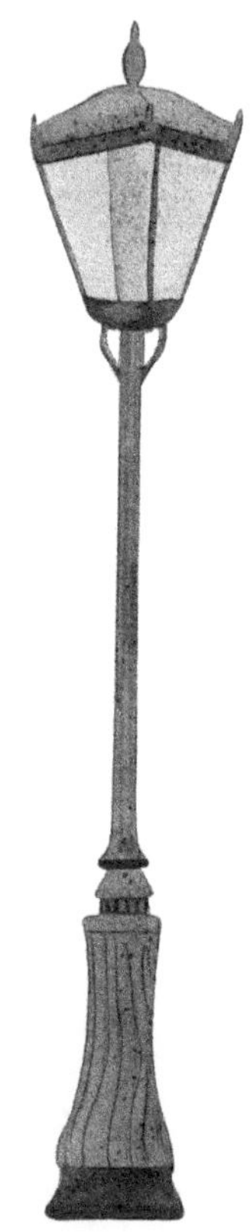

Chapter 1
On Creative Work

Let me tell you a story about me. Or, several versions of me at different points along my journey to discover my creative work and what it means to make it integral to my life.

First, let's visit me at thirty years old: I remember the day when I (miraculously) handed off all four of my young children to the staff at a family camp. I was free for the next four hours… and I had no idea what to do with myself. After ten years fully absorbed in parenting, I'd forgotten who I was when not Mom. I felt this realization as a deep shock and loss. Even though I was happy being a parent, I discovered I wanted something in addition to that role. So, I began trying to fit creativity in the spaces around the edges of my life.

Now see me at age forty: a small business owner running a fledgling publishing business, struggling through the earliest era of crowdfunding, dealing with fulfillment logistics and mailing thousands of packages. At the same time, I had a house full of kids and teenagers, many of whom had special needs, requiring me to advocate for them at school and other public places. My life overflowed with administrative tasks, and my writing energy went to marketing text or social media posts instead of the books I wanted to be writing.

Find me now in my fifties: I have acquired confidence, created publications, and achieved a list of accomplishments that surprises me when I stop to consider them. I live in a house of adults, each trying to launch in their own ways. My business is in transition, adapting to changes in the publishing landscape and to my disabled husband/business partner's changed capacity. I still sometimes struggle to keep creative space clear from tasks that claim my energy, but I have developed skills and practice at finding solutions to each day's problems. I've reached a place where I can look back at the small choices I made along this journey and see how those choices changed my trajectory, helping me arrive where I am now. I can see which choices helped make space in my life so that my creative work had a chance to grow and thrive alongside everything else I wanted to do.

Which brings me to the point of this book: to help you, wherever your starting point may be, arrange the structure of your life and give your creative work a space inside it. Small changes in how you structure your time, physical spaces, tools, or thinking can make a giant difference in your ability to grow creatively and accomplish your own creative work.

> YOUR CREATIVE WORK THRIVES WHEN YOU RECOGNIZE HOW MUCH IN YOUR LIFE REQUIRES CREATIVE ENERGY AND WHEN YOU ORGANIZE YOUR LIFE TO REDUCE THE CREATIVE COST OF YOUR TASKS.

Creativity is Everywhere

Creativity is often narrowly defined both by society and within the confines of our own minds. Artists, musicians, sculptors, poets, and writers may be the headliners when we think of creative people, but to include only those pursuits is to ignore the vast wealth of creative effort that flows out of every human with enough health, resources, and energy to thrive rather than only survive. Creations do not have to be grand in order to qualify. People doodle on whiteboards, chain together dandelions for fun, and build sandcastles that will be erased in mere hours And what is "making friends" except an act of creating connection? All of these things (and so many more) require us to use our creativity. They pull energy from us and give energy to us. They require us to make order out of pieces that were separate.

Creative Cost

Unfortunately, this means that activities like grocery shopping, organizing closets, updating spreadsheets, and doing the dishes also use our creativity. Any time you expend mental energy or physical labor to re-shape the world around you, you are spending creative effort. So many of the daily tasks of life have an invisible creative cost. Grocery shopping, for example, is an hour or more of making dozens of complex, tiny, decisions about what resources to acquire. All those micro decisions draw from the same creative resource that feeds the projects you want to do. Exploring and removing needless creative costs is a large part of what this book is about. For now, it is important to realize how much of your creative energy is absorbed by things that are not your creative projects.

Creative Interference

Recognizing the creative cost of daily tasks leads to the realization of how many things interfere with your ability to work on creative projects. I'm going to bold this next thought because it is important:

Any creative effort you have in your life draws from the same creative source as every other creative process in your life.

Parenting will interfere with writing. Reorganizing your apartment will interfere with art. Building and maintaining friendships will interfere with parenting. That presentation you're putting together for work will interfere with the report you need to file (also for work). And vice versa.

Please don't be discouraged by this fact. All of those activities were already interfering with each other in your life. Once you see what's in competition for your limited resources of time and energy, you will be empowered to make choices, and choosing is itself a creative act. The rest of this book is designed to help guide those choices.

Activities

Creativity Activity 1
Listing Your Creative Costs

Purpose: To help you see how many tasks in your life require creative effort.

Write a list of your creative projects. These are the things you want to make more space for in your life, the reason you picked up this book. This is your *Creative Projects List.*

Now make a list of anything that has you shaping order out of chaos, making a decision, or creating something. Even include items you may not have thought of as creative before, like grocery shopping. It may be a long list, but that's okay. This is your *Tasks With Creative Cost List.*

If you have trouble filling out your *Tasks With Creative Costs List*, enlist someone close to you to help you identify tasks, appointments, and commitments in your life that have creative costs.

Creativity Activity 2
Creativity Analysis

Purpose: To explore your feelings about your creative projects in ways that will help with future activities.

Sit down with writing tools and answer the following questions. Your answers can be long and exploratory or brief according to your preference:

- Which creative projects do you want to have more space for?
- How do you feel about making more space for them?
- If you make more space for creative projects, what are you worried you will have to give up?
- What do you feel guilty about when you spend time on your creative projects?
- What are the specific obstacles, challenges, or frustrations that cause you problems when you try to be creative?

Chapter 2
The Landscape of Dreams

When I was in fifth grade, I wanted to be a lion tamer. I don't remember wanting this, but I have the yellowed assignment paper where my childish hand wrote the details of my desire in answer to the question, "What do you want to be when you grow up?" It was an ephemeral wish — I'd probably attended the circus the previous week. Dreams come easily to young children before they are taught to be realistic and before they learn to fear the hurt from falling short. Most of a child's dreams are improbable (my lion tamer dream certainly was) because a child simply doesn't have the brain development or world knowledge to understand the impossibility of what they passionately want. Adults do. Which is why, to save the child from the pain of disappointment, adults will explain, often in detail, how impossible the dream may be, thus squelching the child's dream.

The sad part is that the adults aren't actually preventing the disappointment, just moving it to now instead of later. When children are allowed to reach for impossible dreams, they grow and learn from the reaching. Often, they move on to new dreams before they even get to the impossible parts, but keep the growth and learning.

Most people grow more cautious as they age. In part because they carry the painful memory of having childhood dreams squashed. The result is often hesitance about having big dreams or attempting to reach them. This is a huge loss. Dreams provide direction and motivation, and reaching for a dream, even an impossible one, is an excellent way to grow. Allowing your dreams to be big, impossible, far flung, is a method of allowing you to also be big in potential. **You do not attain breathtaking accomplishments by thinking small.** You have to dare mighty things. You have to counteract all those voices (many of them loving) who want what they think is best for you, who tell you to be realistic. And yes, some dreams actually *are* unattainable. But, often, long before you reach the impossible part of the dream, you've learned and grown so much that what is possible *shifts*. And sometimes, if the right groundwork is laid, the impossible becomes possible.

> YOUR CREATIVE WORK THRIVES WHEN YOU ALLOW YOURSELF TO DREAM BIG, EVEN IF THE PRACTICALITIES OF YOUR CURRENT LIFE LIMIT YOUR ABILITY TO REACH FOR THOSE DREAMS.

Fifth grade me confidently believed she could become a lion tamer. Thirty-year-old me, mother of four small children, struggled to be anything other than "Mom." I had to remember how to wish for things beyond the necessities of the moment and the needs of others. Remembering how to dream was the first step in getting myself moving.

A cautionary note: if the thought of this chapter or its activities make your shoulders go up or your insides clench, skip lightly over this chapter and continue onward. You may have experienced trauma or injury in having dreams squashed in the past. If this describes you, I recommend continuing onward to Chapter 3, *Priorities*, which is much more about the daily needs of your life rather than the landscape of where you want to go. There are chapters much later in this book that directly address deeper healing.

Emotional Starting Points for Considering Dreams

Before launching into our activities to help you recognize your dreams and the purpose they can serve in your life, it is important to know your emotional starting point when thinking about dreams. See if you recognize yourself in one of the five starting points here:

- **Over-confident and enthusiastic.** The confidently-directed person does not need encouragement to dream. Dreams come easily, often accompanied by passion. What this person needs is a way to sort through and focus their dreams to put the most important ones first. My young lion-tamer self was definitely over-confident and enthusiastic.
- **Bewildered and uncertain.** These people are so practiced at setting their own wants and needs aside to make space for others they've almost forgotten how to want for themselves. This person needs to put conscious practice into allowing themselves to want things, even things that are silly or impractical. Me at age 30 was classic bewildered and uncertain.
- **Injured or frozen.** This state happens when a person is too tired or hurt to think long term or pay attention to long-term dreams. Fatigue and injury activate the instinct to huddle up and hide. The injured or frozen person needs to heal by focusing on what is currently happening rather than steering toward a far-off dream. I've cycled through injured and frozen many times during my life.
- **Mindful or contented.** This state describes those focused on being present in life the way it is rather than pushing themselves to travel elsewhere. They're looking organically at the next step in a discovery process instead of crafting the next step to deliberately move toward a big dream. This state could also be described as exploratory- or interest-driven. A grand plan is not always required for growth. Dreams can be tiny, daily, and close at hand.

- **Deliberately directed.** People in this state have a clear sense of where they want to aim their efforts and which dreams matter most. They often deploy goals as tools to reach their dreams. I'll talk much more about goals later in this book.

If you've read through this list and none of these describe you, you could be a mix of several types or something else entirely. In that case, use my list as a jumping-off point to describe for yourself how you relate to your dreams.

A Taxonomy for Sorting Dreams

So far in this chapter, I've used the single word "dream" as a label for what you want for yourself, but it is useful to recognize that there are different types and intensities of dreams:

- **Guiding Lights.** Dreams you're willing to shape your life around, discarding or deprioritizing aspects of your life that don't support that dream.
- **Wayposts.** Dreams you want for yourself, but you are not be willing to bend your whole life toward.
- **Serendipitous.** Dreams you'll happily collect if they land in your path, but don't want enough to disrupt other parts of your life that are more important to you.
- **Passing Fancies.** Dreams which show up and vanish quickly without disturbing much of anything else.

All of these dream types can fall on the scale from easy to achieve to impossible. Dreams are easy to achieve when you have the skills and resources needed to accomplish them; they're impossible when you don't have those resources or skills (yet). An added layer of complexity is that some dreams require the participation of others. A dream of being happily partnered in life, for example, requires another person to opt in to being partnered with you. So, if your dream requires the participation of others, it may be more difficult to achieve.

The word "achieve" brings me to a point I made earlier, but want to reiterate: **achievement isn't the most important part of having a dream.** The greatest value in having a dream is the direction and momentum it can create in your life. This is true both of grand, nearly impossible dreams, and of tiny, daily, contented dreams. Dreams help us grow, and you can start growing even if your life and creative process feel like they're held together with bailing wire and duct tape.

In Chapter 17, *Goals*, I'll dig into how to plan and build around your dreams. That chapter will help you find ways to make even an "impossible" dream more achievable and guide you towards acquiring the skills necessary to make the impossible possible. Before we're ready to make those goals, however, we must cover practical considerations about relationships, energy levels, and productivity tools.

But even before that, there first needs to be a dream to follow. The following activities aim to help you identify yours. Knowing what your dreams are — large or small, silly or serious, impossible or not — is valuable. And, if you hold them as possibilities in your life, you may discover that what was impossible to you as a young student, might be very easy to grasp ten years and a pile of life experiences later. (It can also be fun to find old lists of dreams from years past and see how they compare to your current list.)

Activities

Dream Activity 1
The Quick List

Purpose: To quickly write down a list which you'll use in additional activities.

Write down a list of your dreams. This list should be written fairly quickly, pulling thoughts off the top of your head. List items without judgment or sorting — it is perfectly fine to put "buy that fancy pen" right next to "develop a life-long practice of meditation." You'll sort the list later; right now, just ask your heart what it wants and see what comes up. Do make sure you include the dreams you have for the creative work you want to do. This is your *Dream List*.

Dream Activity 2
Practicing Dreaming

Purpose: To help people who are uncertain or bewildered open themselves up to the possibilities that dreaming offers.

Choose one or more of the following options as a means to allow yourself to entertain possibilities:

- Create a wishlist at your favorite online retailer and, any time you like something, add it to the list. After accumulating this list for several weeks, see if you recognize any patterns. (Other ideas for list-collecting: Pinterest boards or a physical file folder.)
- Take yourself to a store or farmer's market when you're not in a hurry. Allow yourself to linger over something you admire. You're probably not going to buy it today, or maybe ever, but pausing to admire it lets you acknowledge its wonderfulness and connects you with a part of yourself that feels joy at its existence. If you want, take a picture of the thing and save it to an album.
- Create a folder, either physical or digital, and collect images that make you happy, things you might want.

After you've done one or more of these activities over a span of time (say, a week or two) take a moment to look for patterns in what you have collected. When I collected images that made me happy I found that many of my collected images had an implied journey, a path to take, or a place to travel. I was then able to add "travel more" onto my list of dreams.

Bonus Activity

Make a collage or physical representation of your dreams and display it in a place where it is easily seen.

Dream Activity 3
The Thought Experiments

Purpose: To perform a thought experiment in order to uncover thoughts and dreams you've hidden from yourself. Be prepared to sit and mull over each question to see what it reveals.

Pick one or more of the following questions and either write on them for five to ten minutes or talk through them with another person for the same amount of time. Using the entire allotted time will encourage you to reach past obvious top-of-your-head dreams and instead reconnect with dreams you long ago discarded as impossible.

- What would you do if you knew you would not fail?
- What would you do if you knew all of your bills would be paid for the next five years?
- What would you do if you had no physical limitations?
- How would you spend five million dollars and why? (the dreams are hidden in the why)

Bonus Activity

Once you have finished your writing, revise your Dream List from Activity 1 to incorporate what you've discovered here. Your list can be as long as you want, and the dreams are allowed to contradict each other. You can want to be both a hermit and a socialite. This is the moment for wishing, not winnowing. Realism can sit in the corner for a bit.

Dream Activity 4
Sorting Your Dreams

Purpose: To begin the process of sorting dreams according to emotional importance. (Sorting by attainability and actionability will come later in the book during the discussion on setting goals.)

Now you're ready to sort your list(s) of dreams. It may help to write each dream on separate slips of paper or notecards so you can slide them around as you think about them. I suggest you sort your dreams according to the following categories, but you are welcome to pick your own:

- **Guiding Lights.** Dreams you're willing to shape your life around, discarding or deprioritizing aspects of your life that don't support that dream.
- **Wayposts.** Dreams you want for yourself, but you are not be willing to bend your whole life toward.
- **Serendipitous.** Dreams you'll happily collect if they land in your path, but don't want enough to disrupt other parts of your life that are more important to you.
- **Passing Fancies.** Dreams which show up and vanish quickly without disturbing much of anything else.

Once you feel reasonably confident you know where your dreams fall, put them all into one list and hold onto it. You'll re-visit this list later.

Finding Center

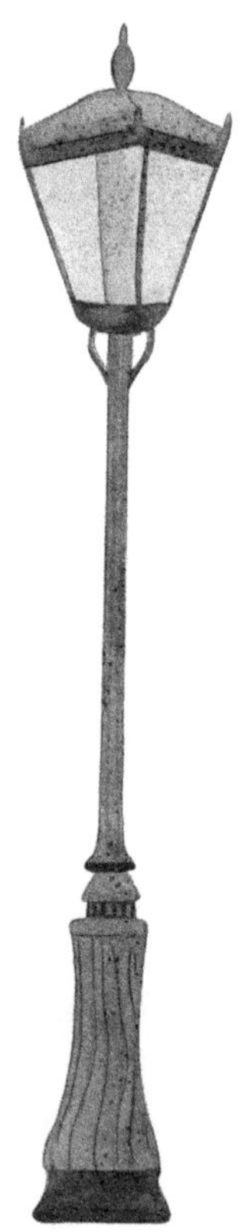

Chapter 3
Priorities

During the years when I juggled professional networking with raising young children, I was involved with a local conference where I taught and connected with other writers. One year, I spent all day Friday at the conference, lingering late into the evening. My children (Ages nine to eighteen) were at home having a movie fest with treats, blankets, and staying up late. On Saturday, I did not have a class to teach, but I did have a ticket for the gala dinner. That morning, my nine-year old snuggled up to me to tell me in detail about the plots of the late-night movies. When he wound down, I asked if he'd had fun and if he wanted another late-night movie fest while I was out again. He shook his head and said, "I'd rather have you, Mom." It was sweet and heart-warming but created a dilemma: I had to choose between connecting with other adults to build my business or staying home to provide stability for my nine-year-old.

This was not the only time I had such a dilemma. They happen constantly to me and, I suspect, to you. A family reunion conflicts with an important work event. The concert you planned to attend for months lands on the only appointment available for an important certification test. Your pet needs to see the vet on the day you're leaving for a trip. In each of these cases, you need a way to make decisions. Having a strong understanding of your priorities can make these decisions less difficult and help dismiss guilt that you're spending your days poorly.

YOUR CREATIVE WORK THRIVES WHEN YOU HAVE A CLEAR PICTURE OF WHAT YOUR PRIORITIES ARE SO YOU CAN PLAN EVERYTHING ELSE AROUND THEM.

Priorities as Identity

One way to approach sorting your priorities is to consider them part of your identity. Priorities define who you are, even to yourself. Sometimes these priorities are given to you by those who raise you and need redefining once you are an adult.

To begin to examine your priorities as identity, express each one in an "I" statement. Examples of such statements are:

- "I will always show up for my kids."
- "I am a responsible child who takes care of my parents."
- "I don't abandon my friends."
- "I always pay my debts on time."

It is possible that in framing your priorities as identity you will discover you've built habits and life patterns around priorities which were once important but are now out of step with your life. For example, "I obey my parents' rules" is a perfectly functional priority for a young child but might need re-thinking for an adult. The person whose priority is "I am a good student who always shows up for class and turns in assignments on time" may have to re-define that priority once they leave school. Priorities shift and change as our lives change. Relationships and self-concepts which once held a central focus in our lives may become peripheral or vanish.

Framing your priorities as identity helps you take ownership over them.

The Priorities of Others

Let's pause a moment and look at the guilt many people feel about not spending their time well. When guilt takes up space in your mind, you have to use energy to push it back or dismiss it. That mental space and energy could be used for other things, including your creative work.

Why, when you're already struggling to make a hard choice, does your brain then make you spend additional emotional energy feeling bad about the thing you chose? Often the answer lies in the priorities and values taught to you by others. The "others" may be parents, colleagues, friends, the trainer at work, or even the article you read stating you can keep your house tidy by cleaning for five minutes a day. Humans are social creatures wired to check behaviors against the people around them. That impulse helps all of us be cooperative members of society; however, in order to be healthy, it must be paired with a strong sense of what is important to you. That way, you are secure in your direction, whether your path goes with the expected flow or against it. Having a strong sense of your priorities is even more important if you have to stand against the flow of social pressure in your life.

The activities in this chapter are designed as a progression to help you separate what is important to you from what is important to others. You probably have priorities that take up space in your life even though you wish they didn't. Often, it is because these priorities connect to something that is important to you. For example: "Attending grad school" may not be important to you, but, because it is important to your parents, it fits under the umbrella of "being a dutiful child," which *is* important to you.

Knowing this, you can start to view some of your priorities as umbrellas. Recognizing how many of the daily tasks of your life fall under the "dutiful child" priority can help you evaluate the full weight of that priority in your life. This idea is more fully explored in *The Big Sort* activities at the end of this chapter.

Juggling All the Balls

This chapter and its activities invite you to examine what is important to you. However, you may still be caught in daily dilemmas where you must choose between two things that are both important, as I was with my son and the conference. By knowing what actually matters, you can use your priorities to make choices about how to spend your hours and energy. In service of those daily, hourly, and minute-ly decisions, it is useful to clarify some terminology:

- **Priorities.** The things you have decided are most important to you.
- **Prioritize.** The action of re-orienting your time and attention to put some of your things before others.

It is entirely possible to know your priorities, but unwittingly prioritize tasks that are urgent, distracting, or easy. All too often, people move through life without being consciously aware of what they are prioritizing. This is how life ends up full of the minutia of daily life while big, emotionally important dreams sit idle.

One of the big tasks of making more space in your life for creative work is to prioritize that work and the dreams around what you hope to create. I'll tackle this problem in multiple ways through the rest of the book, always coming back to the priorities lists you'll make in this chapter. (Which you can adjust as often as you need to! You're not locked in, so don't feel a need to get your priority list perfect.)

I find juggling to be a useful metaphor for the small-scale decision making I do on a daily basis. I have more tasks, errands, and appointments than hours to spend on them. I am a juggler with more balls than hands. My solution is to fling the balls in the air and hope to have a hand free when they come back down. Sometimes I don't, and balls are dropped. This is normal. Over time, I've learned when to let a ball fall and catch it on the bounce. Other times, I don't even catch on the bounce. In times of stress,

I let some balls roll across the room and under the couch. When life calms down, I fish them out and put them back into rotation.

One way to identify your priorities is to notice which balls you always drop to catch other ones. The caught balls are the ones you are prioritizing over the ones you let bounce. But that only describes your current habitual actions. In the following activities I'll help you re-prioritize so you catch balls because they're important rather than because they're urgent.

One important distinction to make is that some balls are rubber and some are glass. If you drop the glass ones, they shatter in ways not easy to repair. This, too, is part of your priorities analysis. When you know which balls are fragile, you can take special attention to always catch them.

In deciding whether or not to attend the gala dinner or stay home with my son, I did a quick juggler's analysis. Both my son and the professional connections were priorities for me. On the first day of the conference, I prioritized the professional event because I had obligations to fulfill to other people and because my son's emotional needs were like a rubber ball I could easily catch on the bounce. But when my son said, "I'd rather have you," my evaluation changed. My son was being vulnerable with me, letting me know that on the second day he was more fragile than the day before. He had a stronger need to be caught and held, while the professional event had a much lower fragility. I wouldn't be letting anyone down if I didn't attend. I stayed home with my son that night, trusting I would have future opportunities to network professionally with the community.

Some balls are rubber, others are glass. There are the things you can't move, things you can. Things that are fragile, things that are not. The state of each of your priorities will shift day to day as you choose what to prioritize. The next chapter, *Identify Your Pillars*, will dig much deeper into elements in your life that can't change and must be worked around.

For now, here are some activities to help you identify your priorities. These activities can get big and deep. Thinking about priorities can get emotional. Feel free to take breathers and even to continue onward through the book before fully completing all of these activities (though at a minimum I recommend making the *Quick List*). Information you encounter later in the book may help you see your priorities in a different way as well. Establishing what is important to you and how that is reflected in your daily life is always an iterative process.

Activities

Priorities Activity 1
The Quick List

Purpose: To create a starting point for the rest of the activities in this chapter and the rest of the book.

Sometimes the top-of-your-head answer is the truest one. Sit down with writing implements or with someone willing to listen to you talk and record the things you feel are the priorities in your life. Don't try to organize them or explain them; just create a list of the things, relationships, and people that are important to you. Did your dreams for your creative work make this quick list? Add those now if they didn't.

This is your *Priorities List*. With this simple list, you can move forward through the book or go deeper using the activities that follow.

Priorities Activity 2
Priorities as Identity

Purpose: To re-examine your priorities in a new and more personal light.

Take your *Priorities List* and convert the list to a series of identity statements as shown in the "Priorities as Identity" section of this chapter. (i.e., "I always show up for my friends.") You may discover that a single priority spawns several identity statements in order to cover multiple aspects of why that line item is important to you. This is your *Identities List*. If you want, you may update your *Priorities List* based on what you discovered while making your *Identities List*.

Priorities Activity 3
The Big Sort

Purpose: To walk you through a process of sorting your Priorities List in a way that makes clear which things are important to you and which things are on your list because they're important to others. It will also help you see what you should prioritize and what you should excuse from your life.

The Big Sort: Part 1

Take either your Priorities List or your Identities List (or both) and write each list item on a separate slip of paper or index card. Create two columns or spaces on a table. Label them: "Important to Me" and "Important to Others." Place each priority and identity statement into one of these columns. When picking where things go, try to let go of any tension you may feel. You don't have to decide perfectly for each card. Nothing is permanent here; the paper can very easily be slid to the other column later if you discover it fits better. Just go with your first impulse and try to sort quickly.

The Big Sort: Part 2

Once you're done with your sort, examine the "Important to Others" pile. Since these things are not important to you, it is time to figure out why they made your list at all. Often it is because they connect to something over in your "Important to Me" column. Reusing an example from earlier in this chapter: "Attending grad school" may not be important to you, but because it is important to your parents, it fits under the umbrella of "being a dutiful child," which is important to you. Add cards for priorities or umbrellas as needed.

Now do some important analysis: How many other things fit under that same umbrella? Is your life overburdened with "dutiful child" tasks? What is the weight of that umbrella in your life? Are there other ways to be a dutiful child without devoting your time to a thing which isn't a priority for you? Perhaps you can skip grad school (which isn't important to you) and increase your participation in family celebrations (which are important to you as well as your parents).

You may discover that some items in the "Important to Others" pile don't connect to any of the "Important to Me" items. Take a hard look at those items, because it is time to ask yourself some questions about these priorities. Why do you need them in your life? How much work would it take to eject them? How much disentangling is necessary, and do you have the ability to disengage?

The Big Sort: Part 3

Now focus your attention on the "Important to Me" priorities. Some of these may now be umbrellas that other items fit under. For this next exercise, treat the umbrella and any priorities you've put under it as a single unit. You're going to further sort this column into tiers, from most important to least. This sorting is based purely on how important items are to you, not how urgently they need to be done nor how often they need to take up space in your schedule. Sort based on where you're at right now, knowing you might shuffle them an hour from now. Since they're on separate papers, shuffling is easy. I recommend using five tiers:

- **Tier 1:** Core elements. Keep forever.
- **Tier 2:** Important.
- **Tier 3:** I like these things.
- **Tier 4:** Meh, maybe I don't care about this.
- **Tier 5:** Disengage. Anything you've discovered you want to excuse from your life.

When you're done with your sort, write down your tier sorting onto a piece of paper and date it. Then scoop your loose papers into a box or an envelope.

Bonus Exercise

Repeat The Big Sort activity a week or a month later and compare your sorts.

Priorities Activity 4
Letting it Settle

Purpose: To give your mind and heart some time to sit with all the thoughts about priorities.

Let the *Priorities List* settle in your brain along with the results of your Big Sort. Then, over the next few days or weeks, do a few things that take you outside the regular patterns of your life. Maybe make time to do one of the things you listed as a priority but rarely make time for. Go for a hike or to a museum. Catch up on the show or book you've been wanting to finish. Break up your regular life patterns a little bit in order to let your mind and heart breathe, then look at the lists again and see how the shaking up has changed your thoughts about the priorities on it. If your first pass on the list was written down, maybe try talking it through with someone. Switching the method by which you evaluate the information can help you see it in new ways.

Priorities Activity 5
Revising the Quick Lists

Purpose: To create a list you can reference during other activities in this book.

Look again at the *Priorities* and *Identities* lists you've created and sorted. Revise your *Priorities Quick List* based on what you discovered so you have a simple *Priorities List* to refer to as you proceed through this book. Do the same for your *Identities List* if you wish.

Chapter 4
Identify Your Pillars

I enjoy watching home renovation shows where they knock down walls and re-make spaces. Watching those shows helps me look at my own spaces in a different way. It was because of such shows that I had a dream to knock down a free-standing pantry that divided the kitchen from the front room in my home. Doing so would give me a larger space to socialize while cooking and eating. However, attached to that pantry was a post that extended from the top of the pantry to the ceiling. In renovation shows there was often discussion about whether walls were "load bearing." I stared up at the post in my house and wondered if the roof would collapse if I knocked it out.

This unanswered question stalled my dream for a long time. Until the day I finally crawled into the attic to take a look. I discovered that the post in question stuck up through the sheetrock of the ceiling and connected to…nothing. The ceiling was holding the post in place, not the other way around.

In contrast, I also wanted to move a door. It seemed pretty simple. I could see where the door was and where I wanted it to be. But once I opened the wall, I discovered that the location I wanted for the new door was definitely load bearing and also the major conduit for electrical power coming into the house. I had to adjust the renovation plan for a different door position.

In both cases, knowing what was structural allowed the work to proceed. In both cases, it wasn't immediately obvious what was decorative and what was holding up the roof. In your life, you have load-bearing structures. It might be the day job paying your bills. It might be the care-work you do for other people. It might be obligations to a faith organization you attend. Or it could be any number of things I haven't listed. I call these structures pillars of your life. Once you know what your immovable pillars are, you can spend your energy working around them and with them instead of fighting against them or resenting them. The pillar in the way can become a feature of the space rather than a drawback, but only after you accept that the pillar must be there.

And, yes, you can make a long-term plan for removing a pillar that you really want gone. In future chapters, I will help you curate your commitments and plan for making changes. But, like my trip to the attic, first you need to know what your pillars are and what they hold up.

YOUR CREATIVE WORK THRIVES WHEN YOU IDENTIFY YOUR PILLARS AND ORGANIZE YOUR LIFE AROUND THEM.

Pillar Identification

Some pillars are obvious because you bump into them often. I've always known that family and my commitment to my faith are pillars I depend on and must always remain in place. I plan around these things when deciding how to schedule my days. Another of my obvious pillars is my self-identification as a writer and a creative person. Just as the tasks and daily demands of writing have to work around family, the tasks and daily demands of family have to work around my being a writer.

Your pillars may not be immediately visible to you. This could be because you've become so used to them you stop noticing them. Or it could be that something becomes a pillar while you're not paying attention. (Because, unlike the houses in renovation shows, the metaphorical house that is your life changes and evolves.) This is why I've built an activity that allows you to take a careful look to find out what is taking up space in your days. Such analysis helped me see how my kids' school schedules were a pillar in my life I had to plan around. No matter what else was happening in my day, I had to arrange my schedule so that I (or someone I trusted) was available at 3pm to pick them up. The school drop off and pick up affected many decisions in my daily life for two decades. I built schedules that depended on it. (For example, planning to do my errands after dropping kids at school since I was already in the car.) That pillar vanished each summer and I had to adjust my life because of that missing pillar.

The Purpose of Your Pillars

If a pillar is to remain in your life, you need to understand the purpose it serves. Your pillars should all be connected to a dream, priority, or identity. If, for example, you realized last chapter that you had "not be homeless" as a priority, then a pillar to keep that priority in place might be "a job that pays the bills." The bill-paying-job pillar might interfere with some of the ways you want to arrange your creativity in the available space. Sometimes you might resent the pillar for getting in the way, but it is also good to recognize that the pillar is supporting the roof over your head, both the literal one keeping off the rain and the figurative one of your life priority.

The good news is that sometimes a single pillar can be load-bearing for multiple priorities. That day job might keep a roof over your head, and it might also provide an avenue for social connection and networking. Perhaps it also helps you participate in your larger community in a way that is meaningful and important to you. It could also be an avenue to learn skills you need. That one load-bearing pillar may support a lot of valuable priorities in your life.

When you understand how having a day job is working in service of your creative dreams, you may resent that day job less. When you stop resenting that pillar for being in the way, you free up emotional energy that is then available to spend on your creative projects.

Another important part of understanding your pillars is to pay attention to whether you have enough of them in the right places to support your dreams and priorities. If you have important dreams and priorities that are unsupported, you may need to add a pillar or other form of support. If, for example, "I am a writer of novels" is a high priority, but nowhere in your life have you made space to write novels, then something might need to be rearranged. Creating support for your dreams and priorities does not always require installing a pillar. You can create support in ways that are flexible and movable instead of rigid and unyielding.

Much of the rest of this book will help you figure out what structures you need to place in your life to allow you the time and energy for your creative projects, so please do not get tangled up in labeling every aspect of your life according to whether it is a pillar or a cabinet, a couch or a rug. You only need a general sense of what in your life must be worked around and what can be shifted or changed. Most people only have a few truly immovable pillars.

You may discover that some of the loadbearing structures in your life depend on other people. Maybe you live with a person who pays the bills for you. Perhaps your priority to "raise healthy, well-adjusted kids" is supported by multiple adults who are committed to the same kids. The existence of other people in your life and living space can either help support the load or create the need for additional pillars — or both. It depends on your particular life configuration, which is why I'll explore your support network more fully in the next several chapters.

It is now years since I crawled into the attic and examined that post. The free-standing pantry is gone, and the door has been moved to its new position. Both of those projects revealed further changes I want to make. (New flooring and cabinets are up next.) This is always the way with changes. Sometimes the work moves fast; other times it stalls. But after you've done the work, you're closer to where you want to be.

Activities

Pillar Activity 1
Working Forward from Your Priorities

Purpose: To see if any of your priorities are unsupported and to brainstorm ways of supporting them.

Start with your *Priorities List*. Next to each priority, write down the tasks, appointments, or habits that work in support of that priority. Mark the ones that feel structural to you. For example, in support of a "get my degree" priority, you might have "attend class" as one task or you might want to write down each class separately. You probably don't want to get so granular that you're writing down every assignment for every class, however.

If you discover a priority that is completely unsupported, think about how you can add support for that priority. Can something you already do also work in support of that priority? For example: you might want to stay fluent in Spanish but aren't doing anything about it. If you're reading a lot of books, perhaps read some of the books in Spanish.

Pillar Activity 2
Pulling from Calendars and Lists

Purpose: To discover if you have tasks or appointments taking up space in your life that aren't connected to your priorities. Also to understand why you've scheduled your life in the ways you have.

Sit down with your tools for tracking appointments and tasks (yes, even if you just use sticky notes on your mirror). For this activity, it is helpful if you start with a blank calendar (either digital or physical) and then fill things in. This will force you to look at how you spend your time in new ways. In order to do this, you can go buy yourself a fancy planner, draw your own grids on blank paper, or create a fresh digital calendar. Choosing a method outside of your go-to habits helps you see things from a different perspective. For example, I use an electronic calendar to manage my life, give me alerts, and help me track things, so in order to see things differently I would do this exercise on a paper calendar and handwrite on it.

In your fresh calendar, record the fixed appointments of your life. These are appointments on your calendar that you can't easily move or cancel, like a class you're taking, meetings you attend, or school drop-offs and pick-ups. You can decide how detailed to be. You might want to write down "working at job" as a single block of hours, or you might want to write down the meetings that affect your job hours. If you are attempting to create windows of creative time in the middle of your day, (like writing on your lunch break), then being more granular might be helpful.

Some people lead lives with few fixed points on the calendar, so the next place you can go looking for your pillars is your daily or weekly to-do lists. If there are to-do items that recur frequently, they're likely either pillars or supporting tasks that maintain a pillar. Create lists for daily, weekly, monthly, and yearly tasks.

With your calendar and task lists in front of you, you can begin to analyze. Ask yourself:

- Do the things with the biggest footprint in your life support your highest priorities, or are you giving a lot of schedule space to things that have less value to you?
- What are you prioritizing in how you spend your hours and does that reflect your listed priorities?
- Based on this information, are there changes you want to make in how you spend your time?

Bonus Activity (Digging Deeper)

Look at each item on your calendar or to-do lists. Ask yourself: Why is it there? For example, you might go to work. But why do you go to work? What does going to work accomplish in your life? Perhaps the answer is, "to pay my bills." You can choose to stop with "paying bills" as a priority, or you can dig a little further by asking why you pay bills. Understanding why you do the things you do helps you keep your daily life in alignment with your priorities.

You may want to pause here to journal or talk through your discovery. That will set it in your mind before moving on to the next activity.

Pillar Activity 3
The Long-Term Plan

Purpose: To sketch out a (very preliminary) plan for changes you want to make in your life.

Look at the lists and calendar you've created in the first two activities of this chapter. If you have identified pillars, tasks, or scheduled items that are obstacles to your creative projects, now is the time to write down a long-term plan to restructure and excuse them from your life. For example, if your current day job leaves you too exhausted or mentally drained to do your creative projects, you can create a multi-year plan to shift to a different way of paying your bills. In the meantime, you can use information from upcoming chapters to help you work around this pillar.

If you can't do a major life overhaul right now (most people can't), it is still a good idea to think through the steps. This is saying, "Someday I want to move that pillar!" without getting out your sledgehammer.

Managing Relationships

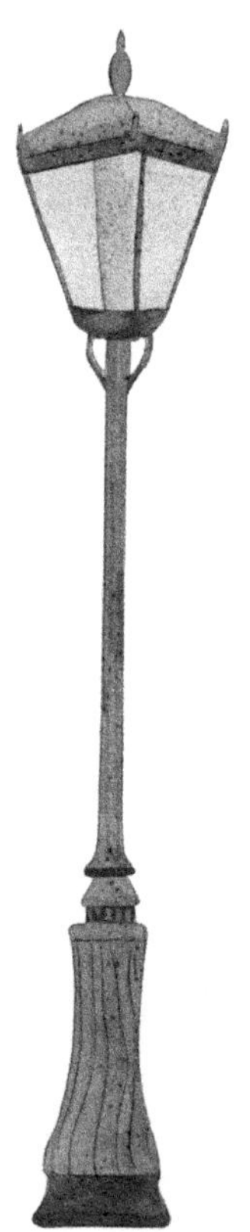

Chapter 5
The Community You Need

In 2004, I was a stay-at-home mother to four young children. My college and high school connections had dwindled to a complete lack of contact. I found myself drifting alone, unsure how to find or maintain friendships.

In that year, two things happened that did not feel transformative at the time but proved to be so in hindsight. The first was that my backyard neighbor moved into the house on the other side of my fence. She brought with her four kids closely matched to mine in ages and interests. She also knew how to be friends with people. I learned so much from the ways she reached out, how she tracked people's special events, and how she created spaces for community and connection to grow by embracing differences. In the decades since, I've continued to benefit from her intelligence and perspective. It was in watching her that I learned how to build in-person friendships.

The second thing that happened in 2004 was that I started writing about my life on LiveJournal. Those writings would become my blog, *One Cobble at a Time*. The act of writing and the connections I made via LiveJournal's rudimentary social media tools were what brought me back to my writer self. Through that online community, I joined a writer's forum which helped me know which conferences and events were worth the effort to find someone to watch my kids so I could attend. Through the LiveJournal community and the online forum, I discovered when submissions were open, found mutual support, and learned how publishing does and doesn't work. I can trace so many of my closest and dearest writer friends back to that first blog and first forum. Moreover, I can trace many projects I've created back to their inception in that community. Without community, I would not have the creative business that has supported my family for two decades.

> YOUR CREATIVE WORK THRIVES WHEN YOU DEVELOP A STRONG NETWORK OF SUPPORTIVE RELATIONSHIPS.

At this point, you may be thinking, "That sounds lovely, but how do *I* get a supportive network?" It isn't something you just find. It is something you build and grow over time. As you gain skills, both the building and the growing get easier to do.

Start With What You Have

Growing a network of connections is like any other project: it needs to start with an honest assessment of what you have followed by a list of what you need to acquire. Begin by answering the following questions:

- Who do you have in your life that you spend time with?
- Who shares your living space?
- Who do you chat with at work?
- Who do you chat with at the coffee shop?
- What are your family relationships like?
- Who do you play games with?
- Who do you interact with on social media?
- Who do you take care of regularly?
- Who takes care of you?

If your network is small, this assessment can feel hopeless and lonely. On the other hand, if you're surrounded by people, it might feel overwhelming. Whatever you feel, remember that what you have now isn't what you will always have. You can change your network.

Once you have a clear idea of the people you already have in your life, you can start to figure out what new people you might need. I would invite you to think less about needing people, however, and more about the roles those people play in your creative life.

The Roles People Play

Identifying people by the roles they play is built into the English language. People are labeled Mother, Father, Boss, Co-worker, etc. Of course, the label Father can't fully describe the relationship between you and your father. However, it gives you a starting point to describe the relationship.

Here are some roles people in your life might take in relation to your creative projects.

- **Cheerleader or Encourager.** This person is always excited about your work and happy you spent time making it. When you feel self-doubt about your project, they tell you it is amazing.
- **Task manager.** This person helps you keep track of the tasks belonging to your creative projects. They may help you schedule your time so creative projects fit in.
- **Accountability partner.** This person isn't necessarily handing out tasks or tracking your time for you as a task manager might, but who checks in to ask "did you do the thing" or to whom you report your progress.
- **Critique partner.** This person helps you look critically at your own work to see the gaps where it might improve. They offer alternate perspectives.
- **Helper.** This person smooths out the path in front of your creative projects They might bring you snacks when you're in the zone, take care of your kids so you can work, pay some bills so you aren't stressed, etc.
- **Mentor.** This person is ahead of you on a path you want to

take. (You can better visualize your creative path if you have some footsteps to follow.) This may be someone you know personally or someone you follow on social media. They may even be a mentor who deliberately teaches you.

- **Student.** This person is behind you on a path you have traveled. Teaching others is one way to solidify what you've learned. Helping others is also a source of purpose. This doesn't have to be a formal role; it can be as simple as you providing information about your learnings.

These are just some examples of roles that people might play in your creative life. There may be roles you need that aren't listed here. I know that when my kids were young, I could have made a parenting-focused list of roles I needed in my life, everything from a babysitter to a friend I could vent to. It is up to you whether you want to think about roles you need for other aspects of your life. You may also want to break these roles down in a more specific way. Under the role of cheerleader, for example, I might list a role for the friend I turn to when self-doubt gets loud.

In coming activities, you will start matching roles to people. It is likely you'll find that one person plays multiple roles. You may also discover that your need for a someone to play a role (say encourager) is so strong you need to spread it out across multiple people.

Remember that in the same way people play roles in your life, you play roles in theirs. If you want healthy long-term connections with other people, then it also is about what they need. You need to think about what roles you can fill for other people. You can find a balance that is beneficial to both of you.

Skill Building

One of the challenges my 2004 self had with building relationships was a lack of interpersonal skills. Most of my friendships in high school and college were the result of proximity rather than effort on my part. Here are a few skill building tips I've since found particularly helpful:

- **Social skills are skills.** Recognize that these are skills and that practice will help you improve. Just because you feel awkward now doesn't mean you have to stay that way.
- **Play to your strengths.** Some skills will be harder for you than others. Lean into the skills that come more easily to you; adapt for the ones that don't. (For example: If recognizing faces is difficult for you, learn to recognize voices or body postures to let you identify people by name.)
- **Names matter.** If you struggle with remembering names, you can practice while watching a TV show with lots of characters. If you realize you don't know the name of a character, either rewind to the moment they were introduced or look it up online. Over time, your brain will improve at grabbing and remembering names.
- **Practice in low stakes situations.** Practice your social skills on grocery clerks and waiters. If you get it wrong, you can walk away with no consequences.
- **Approach with curiosity.** If you get other people to talk about themselves and their interests, they'll think you are interesting. You may also learn things. Ask questions and then ask follow-up questions.
- **Open up.** Getting others to talk is good, but if you hide behind your questions and never share anything about yourself, you are self-isolating. That isolation will wear on friendships.
- **Practice parts of conversation.** You can learn specific conversation openers, extenders and dismounts. It is perfectly fine to rehearse some of these until they feel smooth to you.
- **Social anxiety is real.** Be aware that your perception of how an interaction went may be colored by anxiety or self-doubt. An interaction which felt awkward to you may have been normal to the other person.

Filling the Gaps

You can be very intentional in seeking out the relationships you need. About ten years after I gained my first writing communities, I realized that I had a gap in my support network. I had many author friends, but my closest writer friends were all accomplished novelists while I was still drafting my first novel. I also needed more cheerleading in my life. Additionally, I knew from experience that in-person critique groups could trigger my anxiety to the point of panic attacks even if the people involved were kind. So, I decided to seek out first time novelist friends who were natural cheerleaders and interested in socializing rather than critiquing.

Naming the thing you need helps you be intentional about finding it. In my search I deployed several of the following options:

- **Ask around.** You can ask co-workers, post to social media, or even ask clerks at the grocery store. Just get some practice saying, "I'm a writer looking for a social group. Do you know of any?" Most of the time the answer will be "No." So, then you get to practice saying, "No problem, but if you hear of something, send it my way." What you are doing is planting your need into the minds of other people and making them part of the net you are casting. The net which might lead someone to you. Every time you ask, you practice your asking skills and get more comfortable with speaking what you're looking for.
- **Attend a conference or event.** Pick an event where the sort of people you need are likely to attend. Once you get there, use your "asking around" skills. You should also use your listening skills. Pay attention to what other people at the event say. Maybe there is an online forum you can join. Maybe there are people you can stay in touch with via social media. Collect people for your list of people you know, even though they may not take a role in your creative life at this time. Perhaps you can fill a role that they need.
- **Work dates.** Set up a time where you meet up with other creative people (this can be in person, a group chat, a social

media livestream, or a video call). The purpose of the meet up is to work on your projects.

- **Host a group.** They don't have to share your creative niche. You can have gardeners, painters, architects, and writers all in the same group. Or you can decide that you want to keep your group focused on your specific creative niche. After all this is *your* group, it should meet your needs. The group can be organized however works for you. It can be online or in person. The purpose for this group is for each of you to talk about your projects. Tell the others in your group about your goals and struggles. Listen as they describe their projects and challenges. There is real power in simply talking with others. It helps you clarify what you want and where you are stuck. Expect to spend time and energy building up the group. It may take more than one attempt to find people who will participate with you in building community.

I found the group I needed by asking around, which led to a conversation with a woman I'd known vaguely at church for years. During that conversation, I discovered she was a writer. Then, several months later, her writing group re-organized and she invited me to join. During the meetings, I was able to provide input about what I was looking for and those needs resonated with other people in the group. I felt awkward at first, because my social anxiety is prone to that, but over time the group became a comfortable safe space for me. (Hi, Revisionaries!) This group is now a critical piece of support structure in my creative life.

In my current life, I have online communities, social media buddies, people I visit at conventions, and friends I go out to lunch with. In my twenties I wondered how to have friends. In my fifties, after decades of learning skills and putting in effort, I have more connections than I can easily manage.

Activities

Relationships Activity 1
Identifying Gaps

Purpose: To brainstorm what your ideal creative network looks like and to map that ideal network against the relationships you already have.

Part 1: List of People

Start by writing out a list of all the people in your life. If you wrote a list while thinking through the list of questions earlier in the chapter, you can use that. The point of this list is to really see your relationships. Think about people who are important emotionally, who you see regularly, who live nearby and who live far away. You want people who recognize you when they see you and will respond when you reach out. Your list might end up long or short. This is your *People List.*

Part 2: List of Roles

In a separate list, write the roles that you want in your network. Think about the realities of your life, your pillars, and the tasks required to keep those pillars strong. What could others do to make your creative projects easier? Be as fanciful as you want. Go ahead and list that wealthy patron who pays all your bills so you can create all day. Make sure you also list that more reachable once-per-week accountability partner or childcare partner who tends the kids during writing time. As you continue onward through this book, you may find more roles you want to add to this list. This is your *Roles List.*

Part 3: Matching People to Roles

Now it is time to match your list of people to your list of roles. You can do this as a new list or by writing the people and roles onto separate note cards and sliding them around. If someone in your list of people clearly fills one of the roles, connect those two.

When you're done you may see that you have some roles that are covered more than once while others are sitting lonely. Note the roles that are unfilled in your life and move on to the next activity. This is your *Unfilled Roles List.*

Relationships Activity 2
Filling Your Role Gaps

Purpose: To take steps toward finding people to fill the roles you need in your creative life.

Look again at your list of unfilled roles. Are there people in your life you could ask to take on those roles? Create a new list titled Conversations List and write those names on it. Note the role you hope to fill next to the name. If you already know how to you want to approach that person and are comfortable doing so, go ahead and do that. Otherwise, in the next chapter we'll have a Conversations List activity to help you learn how to have that sort of conversation.

You probably have some roles for whom no one on your list seems like a good fit. Pick one of these roles, then go back in the chapter to review the information above about filling the gaps. Your assignment is to make one attempt to find someone to fill that role. Any attempt, big or small, can count. You might join an online special interest group, post to a forum, host a party — anything that you think might get you closer to filling that needed role. After your attempt, evaluate how it went. Remember that you can succeed at attempting even if the result isn't (yet) a person to fill your role. Each time you try something, you are building skill and experience to apply to your next try.

Relationships Activity 3
Skills Practice

Purpose: To practice social skills in low-stakes situations.

Pick a social skill you want to practice. Make a deliberate effort to practice that skill for a week. For example: you decide to practice conversation, so you talk to grocery store clerks, waiters, and people next to you in line. Can you get them to tell you about their weekend? Can you make them smile? Can you manage to speak full sentences and meet their eyes? If you mess it up, it doesn't matter. In only a minute you can leave and will never have to see them again. You'll have a clean slate ready to try something different next time.

Chapter 6
The Boundaries You Need

Sometimes life shifts without notice. This was the case when I changed from being a full-time, stay-at-home parent to being a work-from-home parent. It happened gradually, business tasks claimed larger and larger shares of my attention. It was two years into the shift before I realized why I was struggling to keep up. To do my work, I needed more uninterrupted time at my computer, yet all of our family habits were built around my being available. The kids and my husband interrupted me constantly. Several of my best beloved people are verbal processors — which means the minute another person is visible, they start talking about whatever is in their heads. This, combined with my workspaces being in shared rooms, meant that I would be trying to draft marketing text while my kid narrated the making of their jelly sandwich.

I had to be available for real needs but unavailable for jelly sandwich conversations. So, we implemented two changes. First, I moved my desk around a corner so that I couldn't be seen and trigger the auto-talk function. Second, I put up a string of lights to indicate, "Yes, Mom is here if you really need her but maybe go make your own sandwich if you can." These two small changes set up boundaries to create a protected space where I was more able to get work done. The changes happened because my husband and I had a conversation where we collaborated to define the boundaries that were needed at that particular moment of life.

YOUR CREATIVE WORK THRIVES WHEN YOU DEVELOP HEALTHY BOUNDARIES WITH THE PEOPLE IN YOUR LIFE TO PROTECT THE CREATIVE WORK YOU WANT TO DO.

Conflict Is Not Bad

Relationships result in conflict. This is not a bad thing. It is merely what happens when the needs of one person collide with the needs of another. You can also experience conflict between your creative projects or between your dreams and the realities of your life. If you are a person who prioritizes people, it can be difficult for you to set aside their needs to work on your projects, but conflict between priorities in your life is normal. Tension between your projects and other aspects of your life is also normal. The process of resolving conflict can actually improve your relationships to other people and with your projects. Just as bridges use tension as a form of support, you can use tension to create a way forward.

Unfortunate Roles People Play

A person may be a huge priority in your life in ways that make your life feel more purposeful and wonderful, but also be a huge drain on your energy. For example, your toddler will not give creative support. They will take up space, distract, and cause damage to your creative projects. Your roommate might be an awesome buddy for movie night, but might want movie night during the only creative time you have available. You may need to defend your creative projects from some of your best-beloved people. They likely aren't engaging in deliberate sabotage, but you still need to defend against it.

As you should define roles you want to seek out and weave into your network, you should also define roles the people in your life inhabit that require you to protect your time and energy. Think about protecting your creative life from the *roles* instead of the *people*.

In naming roles I avoid guessing motivations. Discovering motivations may be a path toward solving the behaviors, but for now I'll define the behaviors themselves and how they might impact your creative workflow, workspace, or work time:

- **Resenter.** A person who resents the time you spend on creative projects. The resentment might be open or it might be passive. This person may claim to support you, but the resentment still exists.
- **Judger.** A person who thinks your creative projects are a waste of time, which may contribute to you also doubting their value.
- **The Confused.** A person who is openly confused by why your creative projects matter to you. This may cause feelings of self-doubt.
- **Criticizer.** A person who evaluates your work to tell you what is wrong with it. Note that this is different than a critique partner, who aims to help strengthen the work. A criticizer tells you the work is bad, broken, or wrong without giving you tools or a path to improvement. Knowing the difference between the two is important because criticizers often masquerade as critiquers.
- **Energy Sponge.** A person who uses your creative energy to serve their own needs. They need you to listen, they need a ride, they need help filling out forms. They need so much and ask you to help them.
- **Source of Chaos.** This person may create physical chaos in your workspace or emotional chaos in your life. You always seem to be cleaning up the messes they leave.
- **The Interrupter.** This person requires frequent attention. While their interruptions may often last only a few moments, they pull your attention away from your projects and disrupt your flow.

There are additional damaging roles people can take in your creative life, but starting with these will help you see how such roles play out in creative projects. Learning to recognize them will give you the tools to recognize others.

Often the people who take on these damaging roles have no bad intent. Your friend who is going through a divorce, for example, needs extra support during a painful transition, yet the hours-long phone calls during your creative time. Put boundaries around when you offer support and when you protect your creative time. Or, you may choose to let the creative project take a back seat to your emotional support role for a while. Either choice is good, so long as you make a conscious decision rather than getting dragged into a support role and resenting your creative loss.

In the last chapter, Activity 1 helped you identify gaps. If you like, you may repeat that activity for the unfortunate roles listed in this chapter, but I find it to be less valuable since you're not trying to make sure you have all of these roles covered. The point of listing these roles is so that when you experience friction between your creative projects and a person in your life, you have some language to describe what is happening.

Necessary Conversations to Reframe Relationships

If you've found someone inhabiting an unfortunate role, you have decisions to make about your next steps. First, you must decide how much effort to put into re-adjusting the relationship with the person in question. Sometimes it is better to gently excuse an acquaintance from your life than to spend a pile of effort to fix the problem. The *Defining Your Boundaries* activity included in this chapter will help you figure out when spending that energy is worthwhile.

Suppose that during the activity you identify a person you absolutely want in your life, but who currently inhabits one of the damaging roles. You need to take steps to reframe that relationship. Resolving the problem may be as simple as having a conversation about the impact of their behavior on your creative projects. But such conversations can be fraught. Here are ten tips to set yourself up for successful conversations:

1. **Pick a time when the person is ready to give you their full attention.** You don't want them to feel interrupted or rushed. For some relationships, scheduling an appointment can be helpful. "Can we go for a walk later? I'd love to talk to you about _____." In other cases, however, doing so may tip the other person into anxiety mode, and they'll come to the conversation stressed instead of open to hearing you out. If your person is likely to pre-think, watch for a time when they're relaxed and open to conversation. Plan a shared activity that makes talking easy, like doing a jigsaw puzzle, going for a walk, going for a drive, fishing, crafting, or something that suits the person with whom you want to have a conversation.

2. **Give them space to think and answer.** Remember that you have had time to rehearse this conversation and your person has not. You may be presenting a pile of new ideas for them to process. It often works better to keep the conversation relatively short and light, with plans to talk again after they've had time to think. The best solutions come from ongoing conversation and change rather than one big reframing conversation.

3. **Think collaboratively.** This is not a case of you deciding what needs to change and expecting the other person to come into alignment. It is better if you begin the conversation with a description of the problem and an invitation to help you figure it out. Even if you're pretty sure what the solution needs to be, start with the problem and listen to how they perceive the situation. People will reject your solutions if they don't see the same problem you do. Make sure you're on the same page about the problem first.

4. **Listen to their problems, too.** Often your conversation will reveal their challenges you can help solve. This is wonderful, because when you trade solutions, everyone feels valued and uplifted. You may want to start your conversation by asking about their struggles first before bringing up the thing you want to change. "You seem to be struggling with ____." is a fantastic

conversation starter. When you offer help with their struggles, they'll be much more open to helping you.

5. **Check to see if their capacities are limited.** Your conversation might uncover that your person is at capacity, unable or unwilling to shift in the ways that you want. This often happens when people are carrying a lot of stress and strain, some of which they may not choose to share with you. Sometimes the conversation reveals that the person can't take on the role you want them to fill, or that they need to stop inhabiting a role that stresses them out. Do people the kindness of believing them when they tell you their limits, whether they express those limits verbally or through behavior.

6. **Give yourself time to process the conversation.** Did the conversation make you feel lighter, unburdened, or more tangled and stressed? Do you think having another conversation would be helpful? Do you still want this person in the role you imagined? Or do you need to set some boundaries to keep them out of a space that you no longer want them tromping through?

7. **Grant them the benefit of the doubt.** There are hundreds of reasons that someone might take unfortunate roles in your creative life. For example, resenters often exist because the person has an unmet need. When their needs are filled, they will have a different relationship with your creative projects. Resentment, bitterness, and jealousy spring from depletion. Putting some thought into causes for behaviors might allow you to be more charitable in your thoughts about those behaviors. Frequently, you will never get to know why, but if you assume the person has good reasons, that can help you be less hurt by their behaviors.

8. **Discuss behaviors, not qualities.** When having a conversation, focus on behaviors, not qualities or root causes. You may be sure the person resents you because they never got enough validation from their own parents, but that challenge isn't yours to solve. Instead, say, for example, "I need you to stop posting snide comments on my Instagram posts. Those really hurt my feelings." And if the mean posts don't stop even after a talk, you may need to use tech tools to set boundaries (like blocking.)

9. **Pick an experiment.** When you and your person decide to try to change how you interact, frame it as an experiment. Schedule a time where you agree to discuss whether the change works for each of you the way you'd hoped. It may also be useful to give the experiment some metrics so you can measure if it is working. However, not all things are measurable. You might have to settle for, "Does this feel better or worse than before?"

10. **Have multiple conversations over time.** These are more likely to readjust your relationship or a person's behaviors than a single big conversation.

Reciprocity

Relationships require a two-way flow. Just as it is important to recognize the helpful and unfortunate roles that other people play in your life, it is also important to recognize the roles you play for them in return. If you require five hours per week of child-free time for your creative projects, what child-free time are you offering to your co-parent so they can also have a break from this super-important shared task? The best solutions are the ones where everyone wins.

Bad Actors in Your Life

Through most of this chapter, I've advocated that you give other people the benefit of the doubt when their behaviors cause problems, but sometimes you have people or relationships in your life with people who actively sabotage or damage you, often in service to their own needs for control or ego. If you have such a person in your life, you may need assistance that is beyond the scope of this book. There are many excellent resources and professional help available for dealing with narcissists, gaslighters, abusers, and manipulators. If you are commonly in contact with such people, you will likely need help to disentangle yourself.

When Conversation Won't Fix It

Even if the person you're struggling with isn't a bad actor, you may discover they can't or don't want to cooperate via a problem-solving conversation. For example, you can't negotiate with toddlers. Some adults are much the same, and you can't negotiate with them either. With adult relationships, you may need to put some boundaries between that person and your creative projects.

Examples of boundary setting include:

- Choosing to keep topics of conversation with that person away from your creative projects.
- Setting time limits on your togetherness.
- Picking shared activities that don't cause friction.
- Not answering phone calls or messages when you don't have the energy to deal with that person.
- Deciding what level of access this person gets to have in your creative life. (See the activities below.)
- Designating blocks of time specifically for your creative projects and not allowing other people to claim or disrupt that time.

Boundary setting can be hard, but is a powerful tool for making space in your life for your creative projects. If you think you'll have trouble maintaining boundaries, see if you can assign the role of "boundary maintenance helper" or "boundary maintenance accountability person" to a trusted person in your life. It can be easier to re-frame the boundaries of a relationship with external support.

If you do discover a person or behavior that needs to be corralled, please don't feel bad. It is okay to have someone as a movie friend and not show them your art. It is okay if your partner doesn't hold the critiquer role; perhaps they're better suited as an enabler or cheerleader. You need some boundaries, even with your closest loved ones. My husband and I have negotiated and renegotiated boundaries endless times as our lives have evolved.

Activities

Boundaries Activity 1
Diagnostic Check

Purpose: To help you determine if a person is a drain on your creative energy.

When you're uncertain whether a person is a creative drain, remember when you last spent time with that person (or pay attention to the next time you interact) and answer these questions:

- How do you feel?
- Are you invigorated for more creative projects?
- Are you doubting the value of your work?

Patterns matter far more than incidents, so a single discouragement is probably a blip. But if you feel discouraged every time you are around a person, you may need to create new boundaries, reframe the relationship, or have a conversation with that person about the roles the person inhabits.

If you decide you want to reframe a relationship, create a new list called the Conversations List and add the names of the people with whom you want to reframe relationships. I'll tackle this list in Activity 3.

Boundaries Activity 2
Defining Your Boundaries

Purpose: To think through where people fit in your circles of trust in your life and creative projects.

Find the list of people and their roles that you made during the *Identifying Gaps* activity in Chapter 5. Re-copy the list to a fresh space if you wish. Then, highlight the people who are pillars or priorities in your life. They get to stay in your life even if they're problematic to your creative projects.

Part 1: Closeness Analysis

Draw a series of rings, starting with a small central one and then adding larger ones surrounding it. I suggest three rings, but you can create more if you wish. Write the names of each of the people on your list into one of the rings. I use the following categories. (Note that I'm not using "family" or "friend" as designators for closeness because blood relation and emotional trust/closeness are two separate things. You may have all your blood relations on the outer ring and your inner rings be full of chosen family or vice versa.)

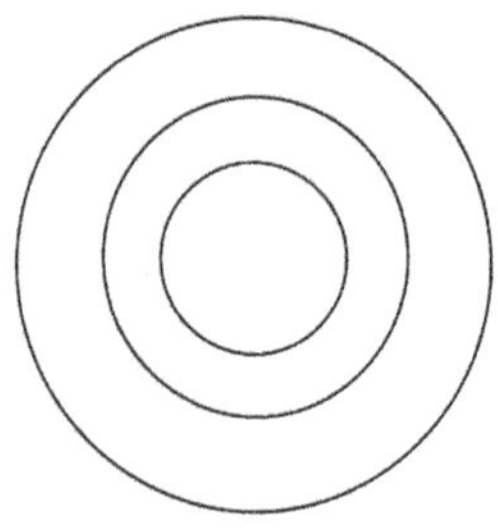

- **Center ring:** These are the people for whom you'll drop everything to help or with whom you love to spend time. They're the ones whose calls you always answer and the people you plan your day around. They are the primary people in your life, your core household (whether or not you live with them).
- **Middle ring:** People you hang out with on occasion. If they call, you'll probably answer, but it might be a day later.
- **Outer ring:** People you run into sometimes but don't make specific plans to meet. Social media friends. Acquaintances.
- **Space outside any rings:** Strangers and people from whom you deliberately distanced yourself.

Pause a moment to look at where your pillar and priority people land on your rings. The further they are from the center, the more you'll need to be careful about the boundaries you set in your relationship.

Part 2: Creative Boundaries Analysis

That first set of rings was about life in general. Now, you'll create a new set of rings specific to your creative life and projects. Again, I use three rings, but you're welcome to create more.

- **Center ring:** People who you trust in the heart of your creative projects. They get to see the messy process. You seek support from them in the mess.
- **Middle ring:** People who sometimes get to see a partial draft.
- **Outer ring:** People who only get to see polished and completed projects.
- **Space outside any rings:** You must protect your creative life from these people. You don't necessarily want them to see or even know about your creative projects.

Again, pause to note where your priority and pillar people land.

Part 3: Comparisons

Take a look at both of your sets of rings. Where are your priority and pillar people in each set? Are there people from your inner rings of life support who are relegated to the outer rings of your creative life? Do you want that to change, or are you comfortable with where people are? For the names where you want to change things, write down those names on a list titled *Conversations List*. You'll do more with this list in the next activity.

If there are no people in the center of your creative life, is that how you want it to be? Do you want to bring some people inside? If you do have a person or people you want to bring further inside your creative life, write their names on the *Conversations List*.

Boundaries Activity 3
The Conversations List

Purpose: To help you plan conversations that create or remove boundaries, and to give you some pre-planned conversation starters.

Take the *Conversations List* you previously created. If you didn't yet make one, use the other activities in this chapter and the prior chapter to help you create one. If you don't have a *Conversations List*, you don't need this activity.

To start, pick the name that feels most urgent or important to you. Take a fresh page and write down a bullet point list of what you want to discuss with them. Think of and write as many points as you can. Then, look at your list and pick the three most important or urgent ones — you probably won't be able to cover more than three points in a single conversation.

If you are anxious about the conversation, practice by writing out in detail everything you want to say. Don't censor yourself.

When you're done, if you've written something you never want them to see, go ahead and destroy that page. I've written myself out of many angry rants and into a more reasonable frame of mind using this technique. Sometimes I've discovered that the thing I thought was bothering me was actually a cover for something much deeper or more important.

If you need to tightly control the conversation, you can read your writing, but you're usually better off putting the practice writing away and just talking.

Review the necessary conversations tips in this chapter when planning to have one of these conversations. Set yourself a timeline for when you'll make a conversation happen. Don't overwhelm yourself by trying to have too many conversations all at once. Have one and then pause and reflect on how it went before launching into the next conversation.

Energy

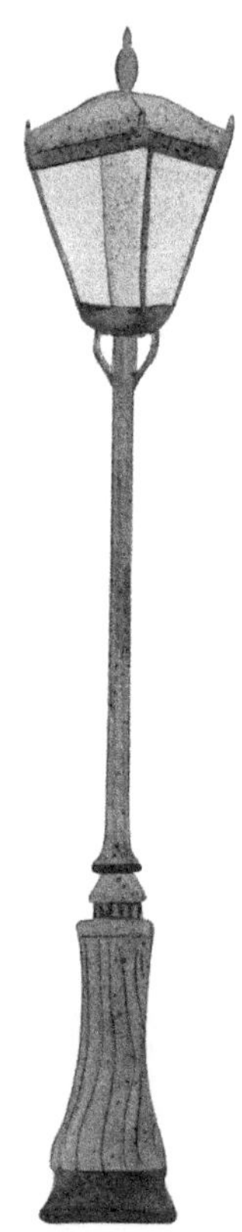

Chapter 7

Managing Mental Load

In January of 2025, the month I was pushing through a revision pass on this book, I was frazzled to the point of burnout. Whenever I sat down to work, I felt pressed for time and often had trouble thinking through what was next. My mind was a desk covered in piles of clutter with only a small space for work. I only had a few appointments on my calendar, but each of those appointments was surrounded with a cloud of anxieties and repeated small decisions. I also held responsibility for multiple simple tasks that needed to be tracked and repeated. The footprint on my calendar was small, but the footprint on my mental desk space was large. I was afraid to push things off my desk for fear I would lose track of them. To make matters worse, my frazzled state created stress in my body, which affected my ability to think, further reducing my available space for creative projects.

Reducing the pile on my mental desk is one way to describe **mental load** (also sometimes called **cognitive load**). Any discussion of how to make space for creativity must address mental load. You need ways to make sure you're not pushing important things off the desk to the floor where they could be lost or misplaced or, for those who have limited working memory or executive function, lost in the void beneath the desk never to be found again. One part of clearing your desk is recognizing that the footprint of a task in your brain differs from the footprint of the task on the calendar. A five-minute phone call might be a quick chore easily checked off the list but might require hours of pre-call anxiety and avoidance with more hours of post-call recovery.

Mental load is often not logical because it is about emotions as much as tasks.

This was my problem in that January revision. I carried a large mental load despite having cleared my calendar. Once I understood that, I was able to make changes to reduce my stress. Understanding mental load empowers you to take action. Reducing your mental load can free up "desk" space for your creative projects even if your calendar looks the same.

> YOUR CREATIVE WORK THRIVES WHEN YOU HAVE A CLEAR PICTURE OF YOUR MENTAL LOAD AND TAKE STEPS TO REDUCE ITS IMPACT ON YOUR LIFE.

I've divided mental load into two parts: **logistical** and **emotional.** The rest of this chapter discusses how to recognize and address elements of each.

Logistical Load

The logistical load of a task is how much you have to hold in your mind and plan ahead for the task to be accomplished. There are three aspects to logistical load, and each can create fatigue:

- **Willpower Fatigue.** Tasks contribute to this if the task requires you to make yourself do it because it is unpleasant or difficult for you rather than flowing easily in your day.
- **Decision Fatigue.** Tasks contribute to this whenever tasks have a decision attached. Even small decisions can have a cumulative effect.
- **Tracking Fatigue.** Tasks contribute to this if you have to remember them or hold them in your mind while doing other things.

When assessing the mental load you carry, the first challenge is to be honest with yourself about how much mental space a task takes up. (Instead of how much mental space you think it should take up.)

Let's take a closer look at each type of mental fatigue and the steps you can take to address it.

Willpower Fatigue

Willpower is the ability to make yourself do things you don't necessarily want to do. It is an exertion against resistance. If you love and want to do something, then getting it done flows naturally and easily. No willpower needed. Using willpower to get stuff done, however, is like holding a weight at the full extension of your arm. It becomes increasingly difficult to maintain. You are much better served by finding some other way to keep that weight in position rather than a constant exertion of energy to hold it there. Willpower is a limited resource you should conserve whenever possible.

Ways to Reduce Willpower Fatigue

Clump your tasks. You need willpower to overcome inertia and get yourself moving, but once moving, you can power through all the tasks with little additional willpower needed. If there are five tasks in your clump, you've used one expenditure of willpower instead of five. This is like stacking things on top of each other on your desk instead of side by side. You can treat the stack as a unit.

Plan around natural conclusions. It takes a large amount of willpower to stop playing a video game and go work on your projects, but it takes less willpower to start working once you have completed lunch. The conclusion can serve as an onramp to your creative projects. You can use a single unit of willpower to get you from one task to another.

Use speed bumps to advantage. You can turn willpower usage to your advantage as well if you put speed bumps and roadblocks between you and any interruptions. If you put software on your computer that prevents you from looking at the internet for a set time, then you've put a speed bump between yourself and getting distracted by the internet. The same can be true for physical space. Something as simple as a closed door can cut down interruptions dramatically.

Make your task more rewarding or interesting. Willpower isn't required when a task is enjoyable, so you can reduce your daily willpower drain by transforming your tasks so that rewards are built in. In children's TV shows and classrooms, they use a "clean up song" to change a chore into a game. Can you do something similar for your task? If nothing else, you can pick a reward that you get to have once the task is done, maybe a food treat or a sticker. Be careful that the reward doesn't require willpower or add Mental Load. If the reward system is hard to maintain, it will likely fall apart.

Decision Fatigue

Each judgment call or decision is an exertion of energy. When you repeat a physical motion, your muscles get tired. When you make repeated decisions, your brain becomes tired and less able to make additional decisions. For example, a preschooler asks their parent for a cracker — which seems like a simple binary question (yes or no), but in order to give that answer, the parent has to evaluate:

- How many crackers are left?
- How many other children might also want a cracker?
- If there are fewer crackers than children, can this child not show off their cracker to the other kids?
- If you give a cracker to this child, how will that affect their next meal?
- Even if this child will be fine eating close to mealtime, what about the other children who may also want a cracker?
- Is this child likely to tantrum if denied a cracker?
- Will that tantrum summon other children, thus expanding the problem?

All of these factors and more have to be considered in ten seconds or less before the child moves to whining or tantrum mode.

That simple yes/no question causes decision fatigue because every single bullet point is a judgment call or decision. This is why caregiving roles such as parenting, elder care, and household management can take up so much creative energy: they require people to make constant micro-decisions all day long.

Just as some people are physically able to lift more weight, some people have more capacity for judgment calls and more executive function than others. In addition, your capacity varies from day to day. Physical fatigue, lack of sleep, illness, burnout, and a host of other factors can all reduce your ability to process and make decisions. Furthermore, some people's supply of executive function is naturally smaller than society expects, which, for those people, may lead to feelings of failure or the use of complex coping strategies that seem odd to those who don't need those strategies.

Ways to Reduce Decision Fatigue

Task clumping. Treating multiple similar tasks like a unit can reduce decision fatigue because you're not making individual decisions about each task. Be careful not to clump two easy tasks into one difficult one. (Yes task clumping is a multi-use tool helping with both willpower and decision fatigue.)

Pre-deciding. If you are faced with a decision that you know you're likely to face again (like the child asking for a cracker), take a little extra time to not only decide for this instance but also for the next one. Create some rules that make future decisions easier. You can decide "no snacks from after 4pm until dinner," and then the cracker question remains a quick = yes/no. Before 4pm, "Sure," after, "No." Weekly meal planning is pre-deciding and can save brain power on a daily basis. Some people simplify their wardrobe so that they don't have to spend energy deciding what to wear that day.

Efficiency of process. The number of steps a task requires impacts the mental load of that task. Hanging a coat on a coat hook by the door takes fewer steps than hanging your coat on a hanger in the closet. Fewer steps means less brainpower spent on those steps. An example is storing cleaning supplies in each bathroom instead of in a central location.

Borrow a brain. Having a second person to help think through the decisions spreads the weight of decision-making across more people.

Tracking Fatigue

Remembering is the invisible work that keeps households and businesses running. Even with calendars, alarms, and tools to help your memory, being the person in charge of the calendar is work, particularly if multiple people's schedules impact the same calendar. I once got a peek at the digital calendar of a friend who has eight children, all engaging in a host of activities. The level of organization and color-coding in the calendar was impressive — and also terrifying. The amount of work she did to keep everything tracked and coordinated was huge, omnipresent, and a daily effort.

Ways to Reduce Tracking Fatigue

Calendars and alarms are your friend. Even if you possess a brain that auto-tracks tasks or even if you don't have much going on, it is still a good idea to get into the habit of using calendars and alarms to assist you in your tracking. It frees up your brain for other work.

Use color. Using color to indicate different types of tasks can help you see what is needed at this moment. If all the appointments for Child One are in blue I can quickly scan through to answer questions about Child One's availability.

Assign tasks to days. If Tuesday is always laundry day, then you can stop feeling bad about laundry or even thinking about laundry --unless it is Tuesday.

Managing willpower, decisions, and tracking is complex. Not all suggestions I've offered will work for you, but hopefully they will provide jumping off points for you to brainstorm your own solutions. For example, folding laundry may be difficult for one person in your household and easy for another. So, assign folding to the person who finds it easy and assign a different task to the other person. Building interdependencies can help everyone have more energy for creative projects or relaxation.

Emotional Load

Emotional load is both the amount of feelings attached to a task and the amount of feelings you carry on an ongoing basis. Those emotions can range from little blips you barely notice to huge feelings (like grief) that swamp everything else. In the Special Cases to Consider section of this book, I'll go over how some of those big emotions impact creative projects. Here, I'll focus on the mental load of daily emotions and how they take up space on your mental desk.

Guilt

Many of the tasks on your lists may come with attached guilt. That guilt sits next to the task on the mental desk, doubling the space the task takes up. The larger the guilt, the more space it takes. When you're able to get rid of the guilt, you have more space on your mental desk to work on your creative projects.

Some Tips for Reducing Guilt

Complete the task. Sometimes completing the task dismisses both the task and the guilt. Other times getting the task done doesn't remove the guilt from your mental desk, so you have to manage it separately. Managing that residual guilt may be as simple as excusing yourself from feeling guilty about the task. "Laundry" is just dirty clothes or clothes that need putting away, not a referendum about your value as a human being.

Dig deeper into the why. Digging deeper to find the why of your guilt may help prevent the guilt from returning when the task (or a similar one) cycles back onto your list.

Put unfinished projects away. If projects are sitting out, you will feel guilty about them. If they're carefully stowed, you can come back to them later and you don't have to feel guilty every time you see them.

Review your priorities list. Where does the guilt-inducing task fit on your list of priorities? If you did something more important, let go of the guilt about the task you didn't get done. You made good use of your limited available energy. If you are regularly doing tasks not on your priority list while tasks related to your priorities aren't getting done, you're out of balance, and the guilt is alerting you to that imbalance.

The Ripcord Task

Some tasks seem small, but when you take them on, you discover they're tied to other things, some of which expand explosively. During my frazzled January, I discovered that dishes were a ripcord task for me. Any time I started to clean dishes, I thought about how I was only doing them because another person hadn't gotten them done. That thought led to more thoughts about how those people weren't getting things done because they were struggling in some way. Which led to thinking about the amount of struggling my people do and how long they've been struggling. From there, it was only a short step to anger and frustration that they weren't doing more, grief for their struggles, or hopelessness because the struggles never seemed to end. A simple 10-minute chore always made my mood worse. And it was a chore I had to face almost daily.

Disconnecting the Ripcord

The core problem of a ripcord task is its connection to a big pocket of emotion. The way to defuse it permanently is to resolve that big emotion. You can do that through healing your emotions, therapy, or shifting your perception of the task. This sort of healing has a creative cost, but — hopefully — once done, you don't have to do it again.

Until you can do that healing, you may need to restructure your approach to the ripcord task so it doesn't yank on all those emotions. As a short-term solution, I started distracting myself with a show or podcast while I worked. This prevented a brain spiral while my hands were busy. I also held a family meeting to better balance the house-keeping load. Another solution would have been to hire help.

Anxiety

All people have anxiety to some degree. Anxiety, in any amount, can be a huge contributor to your overall mental load. I have a brain that, if unchecked, will create a detailed contingency plan with diagrams and lists for any imagined disaster six months in the future. Anxiety wants me to pre-plan every conversation before I have it, and then it wants to endlessly review and rewrite conversations that happened weeks (or years) ago. All the time and energy I spend on pre-planning and post-mortem dissection is time and energy I do not have for creative projects.

You can see my anxiety in action with the story of the cracker conundrum above in the "Decision Fatigue" section of this chapter. Not everyone experiences a cloud of possible outcomes for every simple question, but I do. Anxiety is a thing I must consciously manage. There are many available strategies and therapies for managing anxiety. I recommend seeking them out if anxiety is a regular problem for you. In the meantime, give anxiety some boundaries so it takes up less creative brain space.

Ways of Reducing Anxiety

Anxiety will lie to you. As Dawn Heubner said in her TED talk, 'Rethinking Anxiety: Learning to Face Fear:' "Our thoughts are just our thoughts, not necessarily true, not necessarily useful." Once you recognize that just because a thought arrives in your head doesn't mean you should accept it. You can learn to separate out anxious imaginings from useful thoughts. Then, you can set the anxious imaginings aside, to be considered at a time and place of your choosing, rather than letting them frolic through the middle of your day.

Learn to spectate your thoughts and emotions. In a sports stadium, the spectators in the stands have a much better view of what is happening on the field than the players do. The players can only see what is right in front of them. When you're in your thoughts and emotions, you are like a player on the field. When you spectate, you metaphorically step up into the stands and watch your thoughts and emotions with some distance. That distance allows you to make decisions about what to do next instead of simply reacting to what is right in front of you. Spectating can look like the following:

"Wow, I had a strong reaction to that; I wonder where the reaction is coming from?"

"Did I actually make a fool of myself in that conversation, or is that my anxiety lying to me?"

You can learn to spectate by analyzing situations after they've happened, either by journaling or by talking them through with a trusted friend or therapist. As your skill at observing grows, you can get to the point where you can spectate thoughts while they're happening. Over time you gain more skill at recognizing and dismissing anxious thoughts in the moment they happen.

Dismissing anxious thoughts is an exercise in willpower, which is yet another source of mental load. Rather than just expecting yourself to push away the thought and hold it there, you may need to actively distract yourself. This is what I was doing with my distractions while doing dishes. You can do the same. Play music or a podcast while you work; there won't be space for anxiety to spin. Change locations in the hope that you can leave the anxious thought behind. Take a break and do something fun.

Anxiety can activate your autonomic nervous system. This is the system which floods you with adrenaline and other blood chemicals so you can fight or flee. When you marinate in anxiety, your body reacts the same ways it does to a physical threat. Blood pressure and heart rate increase, preparing you to fight or flee. For some people, a stray anxious thought is merely that. For others, that thought comes with a surge of adrenaline and panic. Logic can tell you there is no emergency, but your body is still filled with emergency chemicals. Anxiety is trying to hijack you. It takes significant medical and therapeutic help to learn how to manage those hijacks if they happen to you regularly.

Establish a worry time. When you have a persistent source of anxiety, pick a specific time when you will address worries. The frequency of your worry time will depend on the shape of your anxieties and the patterns of your life.

For me, finances are a huge anxiety trigger, so I set aside time on Fridays to go over my accounts and double-check everything. At the end of my accounting time, I take a moment to pause, breathe, and remind myself that (barring any big expenditures) everything is fine for the next week. That way, when my Tuesday brain wants to fret over whether I'll run out of money three months from now, I can tell it firmly, "I'm fine today; I'll check for that on Friday." In between Fridays, I have to trust that the me of last Friday knew what she was doing and that the me of next Friday will handle whatever has come up in the meantime.

You may need separate worry times for different anxieties. I don't put my parenting worry time on Fridays. Instead, it is addressed irregularly when the parenting worries have accumulated enough. One of my children took "worry time" a step further by crafting worry dolls from bits of wood and string. When worried, they would craft a worry doll to hold that worry for them. Then in the evening before bed, they would look through that day's collection of worry dolls and put them to bed before going to sleep. It was an adorable nightly ritual and it helped calm the child's feelings.

Think through the worst-case scenario. Instead of stopping the thought, follow it to the terrible end. Take a moment to look at the result and see if it seems likely to you. Start planning exactly how you'd handle that worst-case scenario. What would you do? How would you recover? What would your next steps be? Often, by laying out a plan for the absolute worst case, you can let go of creating a contingency plan or all of the medium to good outcomes. Test this worst-case planning and see if it lowers your stress or raises it. If you find it increases your anxiety, don't engage in this exercise again.

Activities

Mental Load Activity 1
Task Analysis

Purpose: To take a close look at your tasks and identify those creating the largest mental load.

Make a grid with six columns. Label the columns: Tasks, Willpower, Decision Fatigue, Tracking Fatigue, Emotional Load, and Anxiety. In the Tasks column, write down four tasks you do regularly whose process is smooth. Then, write down four tasks that feel hard, heavy, or guilt-inducing. You almost certainly have more than four tasks of each type, and you're welcome to do a full analysis of every task you can think of, but four of each should let you see patterns of what is difficult for you.

In the remaining columns assign each task a number from 1-4 based on how hard the task feels to you. If a task requires a lot of decision making, it should get a 4 in the Decision Fatigue column. If it requires little, give it a 1. Go with your first instinct rather than trying to consider the perfect number. Repeat for all the tasks in all the columns.

Are there patterns in the result? Are the difficult tasks hitting the same problems or different ones? Based on the patterns you see, form an experiment to tackle one form of mental load in your life, the one with the highest numbers. Pick one of the strategies earlier in this chapter for reducing that form of mental load and try it out for a week.

Mental Load Activity 2
Establishing Worry Time

Purpose: To practice limiting when and how much anxiety is allowed to impact your day.

Pick a particular anxiety or worry, then pick a specific time when you will address it. During your worry time, follow these steps:

1. Free write or talk through your fears about the worry.
2. Take at least one small action toward resolving the worry.
3. You are now excused from worrying about the thing until your next scheduled worry time.

Mental Load Activity 3
The Worst-Case List

Purpose: To realize that when you think through the worst-case case, everything else feels manageable.

Pick something you are worried about and free write about the following:

- What would you do in the worst case?
- How would you recover?
- What would the next steps be?

Or, if you want to be less structured, let yourself ramble on paper about what you are anxious about and why. See what emerges. Ask yourself "Why?" questions about your fears to see if you can find the source of the fear. You could also ramble to a sympathetic listener if talking is easier for you than writing.

Mental Load Activity 4
The Guilty Tasks

Purpose: To help you look at tasks that make you feel guilty and examine options to shake loose that guilt.

Make a list of the tasks you feel guilty for not doing. Then, pick one of the following:

- Compare this Guilty Tasks list to your *Priorities List*. If the guilty tasks aren't priorities, excuse yourself from feeling bad about them. Are clean baseboards an important priority in your life? No? Then stop feeling guilty about them; you're doing the things that matter to you.
- Arrange a time with a friend or housemate to pool your list of stupid, guilt-inducing tasks and band together to get them done. Sometimes having another person is all it takes to turn a task from impossible to possible.
- Write yourself a permission slip or excuse note à la your school days. For example: "[Your name] is hereby excused from cleaning baseboards and is further excused from feeling guilty about cleaning baseboards." Putting the words in writing can really help you absorb them.

Mental Load Activity 5
Building Reward Systems

Purpose: To brainstorm ways to add rewards to tasks.

Look at your task analysis from *Mental Load Activity 1* and pick one task that requires willpower to make yourself do it. Is there a way to transform the task to be more inherently rewarding? (like singing the clean-up song while doing the work?) Is there a reward you can give yourself once the job is complete?

Pick a reward system and use it for a week. At the end of the week, pause and evaluate whether the reward helped or if it just added to your mental load.

Chapter 8

Ebbs and Flows of Energy

I was in my early twenties when I learned an important fact about the realities of creative work. My friend, Dave, a computer programmer, often struggled to stay focused and productive through his eight-hour workday. As he attempted to fix this problem, he noticed a pattern. In the mornings, he felt sharp, focused, and capable of solving complex problems. But after lunch, he felt none of those things. Hours felt wasted as he struggled through problems that would have been easy with his morning brain.

With this realization, Dave made a small change to how he worked. He used the morning hours to solve complex problems, but he stopped spending morning time implementing those solutions. Instead, he wrote the solutions on Post-its and lined them up around the edges of his monitor. When he returned from lunch feeling sluggish, he would stare at all the Post-its and think, "Wow, the guy who sits at my desk in the morning is really smart." Then, he would pick up one Post-it, and think, "Well, that one is a small task. I can probably do that." One by one he would follow the instructions he left for himself in the morning, doing the much less demanding work of implementing solutions through the afternoon.

From Dave's story, I learned that some parts of my creative projects require me to think clearly and problem-solve. Other parts are tedious but simple. I've learned to schedule complex work when I am Smart Sandra and simple work for when I am the opposite. I have to match the work to my brain mode, complex or simple.

YOUR CREATIVE WORK THRIVES WHEN YOU PLAN YOUR CREATIVE WORK AROUND THE NATURAL EBBS AND FLOWS OF YOUR ENERGY LEVELS.

Your Daily Patterns

Dave's story describes a daily cycle with high creative energy in the morning and a lull in the afternoon. You may have similar energy patterns, though the exact timing of those energy highs and lows varies from person to person. A common pattern is: good energy in the morning, a lull in the middle of the day, and a second wind in the evening. Another common pattern is to be sluggish all morning with the brain kicking into gear in mid-afternoon. "Early bird" people do their best and clearest thinking first thing in the morning, while "Night Owls" have their clearest thoughts at the end of the day.

Figuring out your natural daily pattern for energy is helpful. If you only have one hour of creative time per day, you don't want to schedule it during the time of day when your body wants to take a nap. You can attempt to ignore your daily patterns if you wish, but pushing against your natural rhythms has a higher creative cost than working with them. Natural night owls are smart to take afternoon and evening classes whenever they can. Similarly, they'll have an easier time creatively if they stay up late to work on projects instead of trying to get up early for them.

Keep in mind that while the sun and clocks run on a strict 24-hour schedule, some people's natural sleeping and waking rhythms run on a 22 or 26-hour cycle rather than 24. These people tend to accidentally drift free of clocks, becoming nocturnal or awake at hours when others aren't. I know writers who take advantage of this, putting their writing time in late at night or early in the morning when they won't be bothered by others. If, however, this natural inclination of your body creates problems, you may want to spend some time finding ways to keep yourself tethered to the schedule of hours everyone else uses.

Another daily pattern that must be managed is the need to eat. Dave's lunch was necessary to keep him alive during the day, but digestion also contributed to that afternoon lull. Bodies have different ways of metabolizing foods. Some people are more prone to sugar or carbohydrate crashes. The food you eat can impact whether you have sustained energy throughout the day or if you crash part way through. Since one person's healthy diet can be harmful to another person, I'm not going to make recommendations for particular foods, but I recommend observing how your body interacts with foods. Eating the right foods at the right times can help you have more flows and less ebbs in your energy levels. Eating right really does help.

Regular exercise is good for you and can improve your energy levels, but exercise can feel like yet another thing taking your time, leaving less of it available for creative projects. But perhaps you can go for a walk or exercise when your energy is low. Sometimes physical activity can restore your ability to do complex thinking. You could carry a notebook or recorder to catch the ideas that come to you while exercising. That way, exercise becomes an integrated part of your process instead of a distraction.

Sleep is another daily pattern to consider as part of the planning structure around your creative projects. Planning around sleep starts with knowing how much sleep you're getting, especially if you routinely struggle with disrupted sleep. I used to create a graph to track my baby's sleep, and I was surprised at how quickly I could visually see patterns for my child's disrupted sleep. Seeing the patterns helped me make decisions about when to schedule naptime or bedtime. Keeping the graph always taught me something, even when I thought I already understood what was happening. Seeing the pattern gave me power to change the pattern. Tracking your sleep for a few weeks, either old school with graph paper or higher tech with a wearable tracker, might show you its patterns.

If you build your daily creative life and supporting structure by ignoring the needs of your body, your systems will likely fall apart when your body fails. You are better off creatively if you build a life with a pace and structure that takes your physical needs and limitations into account. A constant over-production-crash-and-burn cycle can destroy your physical health.

Abusing your body is a path to acquiring disabilities. The bill for long-term stress eventually comes due. Since disability comes for all of us sooner or later, I discuss working with and around disability more in Chapter 19, *Your Access Needs* and Chapter 21 *Health Challenges and Creativity.* What matters for now is accurately determining your current energy levels, patterns of high and low energy, and needs for physical rest and recuperation. Try to work inside the bounds you have, even if you wish they were different.

If large amounts of fatigue are a daily occurrence for you, a medical appointment can help you find causes. Conditions like sleep apnea, low iron, and blood sugar can have a significant impact on daily energy levels. An annual wellness check is part of the due diligence on keeping your body running so you can do all the creative projects you want to do.

Annual and Longer Patterns

Alongside the daily patterns of your energy levels, you must plan for longer-running cycles of energy and fatigue. Some people have bodies and brains that respond to the annual cycles of available daylight with mood and energy changes. Some bodies want to hibernate in the winter; others come alive in the cold air. When looking at the creative projects you want to accomplish, the work will flow more smoothly if you schedule tasks according to higher and lower energy times of year. Light is not the only annual cycle. After years of experience, I know not to schedule any focused or sustained effort between Thanksgiving and New Year. That season is a very brain-frazzled one for me. I can manage short bursts of focus but not ongoing sustained attention.

You may have to do some self-observation to find your annual patterns. You can also look through old text messages or ask your friends and family if they notice any cyclical patterns in your life. If you are a person who posts to social media, scanning old posts might help you find annual energy patterns in your life. There was a time when I carried a trauma that made me depressed from mid-January until March. I only recognized the pattern when I read through old journal entries and compared the sorts of things I wrote in January every year. One of the ways I pushed back against my winter doldrums was planting a hydroponic garden timed to bloom and grow in the darkest part of winter. That way, I used some of my fall energy to proactively be nice to my low-energy winter-self who would need a pick-me-up.

Another cycle that can cause energy highs and lows is the current stage of your project. There are parts of your creative projects that interest and energize you while other parts need to be pushed through. Many a novelist has lamented the "messy middle," and many an artist has been discouraged by "the ugly stage." When you are new to your creative projects, these "slog through it" portions can feel like the project is dead, and you may be tempted to abandon it for a new, shinier idea. When your project hits a slog point, it takes more work to push it forward. Creators with more experience begin to recognize the patterns of these project low spots. Your support network can be instrumental in helping you recognize when you've hit a project low. I have a writer friend who was complaining to her spouse about the impossibility of the plot she was wrestling with. Spouse said, "Are you at the 3/4 mark?" Yes, she was. Spouse nodded. "You always say this at the 3/4 mark."

Be compassionate with yourself about the energy you have, especially in the dozy-nappy part of the day in the month that is depressing for you or on a part of the project which is a slog.

Activities

Energy Activity 1
Sorting for Complex and Simple Tasks

Purpose: To take a look at the tasks specific to your creative projects and to sort them according to whether they require simple or complex thinking. This sort will help you match the parts of your creative projects to your available energy levels.

Write down the tasks and work of your creative project in list form. For example, a novel might require worldbuilding, brainstorming, outlining, drafting, and revising.

Look at this list and consider the following questions:

- Which of these jobs are ones you have to do when you have high focus and problem-solving ability?
- Which of the jobs can you do when your brain is more in simple mode?

Create a second column and write "simple" or "complex" next to each of these tasks. When you have time available for your creative projects, pause to consider this list and match either a simple or complex task to the brain you have available in that moment. You are now empowered to make choices about spending your available creative time. Don't waste your smart brain on simple tasks.

Energy Activity 2
Tracking and Graphing

Purpose: To track some of the daily patterns of your life to see if there are patterns you can use to advantage in your creative projects.

Pick a tracking method. This can be done via a tech tool like an activity tracker or by simply using a notebook or graph paper. Ideally, your method will result in a graph or other visualized representation which allows you to see multiple days of data at once in a way that lets you recognize patterns. Pick one or more of the following to track:

- **Sleep.** Look for patterns in your waking and sleeping times. You may also want to mark when you feel sleepy or low energy — like that afternoon lull.
- **Exercise.** Pick a physical activity (for example, going for a walk) and experiment with its effect on your energy levels and mental focus at various times of the day. Does walking first thing in the morning give you a longer-focused work brain? Does going for a walk at lunch gives you a reset and refocus moment at midday? Does that midday walk make the afternoon drowsy worse?
- **Food.** Keep a food log and note how what you eat affects your energy and creative focus. Sometimes, people try to compensate for lack of energy by eating or drinking something (often caffeine). Experimentation can help you identify whether those pick-me-ups are as helpful as downtime.
- **Mood.** Use colors and a calendar to track your mood to see if there are patterns in how you feel from day to day.

If there is a pattern, two weeks of records should make it clear. Tracking for two weeks will also let you see how weekends affect you. Seeing the pattern empowers you to make decisions about the pattern. If you're looking for large-scale patterns, make sure your tracking method is one you can sustain over a long period of time.

Energy Activity 3
Scanning Your Calendar for Patterns

Purpose: To look for annual (and longer) patterns that may affect long-term planning for your creative projects.

Sit down with your social media, journal, or photo album. Scan through a single month across multiple years. For example: look at 3-5 years' worth of September posts, journal entries, and pictures. Do you see any patterns in your life and mood in September? Repeat for other months. If you don't have posts, pictures, or journals to scan through, then beginning some sort of log now might give you data in the future. It can be simple notations or long form journal keeping.

Alternate version: sit down with a person you've known for years who you interact with regularly. Ask them if they notice any seasonal patterns in your behavior and energy.

Chapter 9

Depletion and Replenishment

Inside the Uinta National Forest is a place called Cascade Springs. The name is self-descriptive, as this is where all the water accumulated by the rain and snow on the mountains bursts forth in a multitude of springs, streams, ponds, and small knee-high waterfalls called cascades. In an area that is largely desert, this abundance of water is unusual and gives homes to wildlife not found elsewhere.

I've visited Cascade Springs on many occasions. Sometimes it is closed because so much water has overrun the walkways and trails. Other times, drought hits hard. During one of my visits, I'd come specifically because I felt over-tapped and wrung out. I was seeking an abundance of running water, but that year was drought, and the cascades were nearly dry. The dried moss and cracked earth echoed my own depletion as I walked the trails. It was sad to see, but nothing can make the water flow unless the reserves are there.

When discussing creativity, people often speak of returning to the creative well, refilling themselves, or pouring themselves out. In the metaphors, there is an acknowledgment that creative efforts use a resource which can be depleted, just like the cascades can dry up. Your reservoir of creative energy comes from the places you go, the people you talk to, and the things you experience. It gathers, not in a single giant pool, but in a deep aquifer made of interconnected reservoirs with dozens of inflows and outflows. Your goal is not to hoard this precious resource and miser out small portions only for your work. Your goal is abundance, where the outflows benefit yourself and others, and the inflows ensure you never run dry.

YOUR CREATIVE WORK THRIVES WHEN YOU ESTABLISH A HEALTHY BALANCE BETWEEN THE INFLOWS AND OUTFLOWS OF YOUR CREATIVE AQUIFER.

Inflows and Outflows

One of the most common questions I get when giving presentations is, "How do I make myself write (or draw, or design, or craft) when I come home from work completely drained?" The question is vital, but it needs to be paired with a matching question: How can you come home from work less drained? Understanding your aquifer means that any time you identify a pinch point where you don't have enough flow, you need to look upstream. Sometimes the solution to a lack of flow in one place is stopping up half a dozen small drains upstream. Or the solution may be adding an inflow in a critical place. Or it might be diverting flow into your creative projects before the day job has a chance to absorb it all.

I remind you here of what I said in Chapter 1, *On Creativity*: **Any creative effort you have in your life draws from the same creative source as every other creative process in your life**. Every creative effort draws from your aquifer. Some activities will draw from one pool and feed directly into another. Others will expend energy as an outflow. For example, attending a conference or event may be a huge outpouring of energy that leaves you tapped out and depleted for days afterward, but also be a massive inflow of connection, brainstorming, and motivation. In contrast, a critique group that is supposed to feed and support your creative projects may instead weigh you down with administrative burdens and interpersonal drama. What was supposed to be an inflow ends up being a drain.

The good news is that, unlike the mountain (which must depend on water falling from the sky) you can arrange inflows for yourself, and you can sometimes control your outflows. The other good news is that, with attention, it's possible to notice the early signs of depletion and course correct before the flows dry up. Recognizing depletion early starts with an understanding of how depletion manifests for you.

Observation and Inquiry

To identify your own inflows and outflows, you'll have to observe your activities and feelings in the context of your daily life. Once you've observed depletion, pause and ask why you think it is happening. Suppose you arrive home from your work day too depleted to work on your project in the evening. Pause and observe the feeling, name it out loud, then reflect on what happened to contribute to your depletion. Are you more depleted when you have many meetings? Then meetings might be an outflow for you. Are you less depleted on days when you complete big tasks? Task completion might be an inflow for you.

You can run the same sort of observation around your creative projects. If you have a really good creative day (or week) take a moment to look at what happened before. Did you meet up with a friend? Go out to a movie? Renew your physical activity? Pick up a spiritual practice? Cancel an appointment? Was there something identifiable that refilled your well so creativity flowed naturally from it? You might not be able to identify this from a single good creative day, but over time, you can begin to learn your inflows and outflows.

Another thing to watch for in your observations is whether an outflow in one place is an inflow in another, as mentioned above in the example of a writer's conference.

As you begin to know your inflows and outflows, you will be empowered to make decisions to adjust your flows.

Identifying Depletion

Some common signs of operating from a depleted state are:

- You're asked how you're doing, and your first thoughtis "tired" or "okay" instead of "good" or "great."
- Binge-watching or binge-playing games.
- Oversleeping or insomnia.
- Feelings of exhaustion, fatigue, or overwhelm.
- Overeating or not eating enough.
- Feeling flat or disconnected from your emotions.
- Overreacting to small things.
- Flare-ups in physical health problems.
- Flare-ups in mental health problems.

These are just symptoms and, like a fever, could indicate different depletions for different people. You need to figure out what these behaviors mean for you in your life.

For me, binge watching means I've depleted my executive function, and I need to rest from making decisions in order to replenish. When my executive function is not tired, I get bored with endless watching and do other things. However, this is different for some of my family members with ADHD, where binge-watching seems to be an integral part of the creative process.

Feelings of exhaustion and overwhelm mean I've packed my days too full for an extended period. For some of my loved ones, these feelings happen when they have to task swap too often.

Overeating means I'm short on sleep or energy, and I reach for calories to keep me moving. Overeating may have a different source for others. For a man I know, food is a source of serotonin joy, and he reaches for food when depressed.

And that is only looking at the "common signs" list I created. You may have signs of depletion specific to *you*. It will take some time and practice for you to learn your signs of depletion. You may also find some early indicators that let you prevent full depletion. My early indicators tend to be small: emails that should have had quick replies which sit unanswered, friends I think of reaching out to but don't, piles in my house that accumulate because putting them away feels like just one effort too many. These indicate I haven't been tracking at my usual efficiency and need to increase my inflows and decrease my outflows.

Reducing Outflows

"Reduce your outflows" is simple for me to say, but the reality of doing it is far more complex. Many of your outflows are necessary. Food preparation and cleanup may be draining, but if you don't eat, you don't have the energy for creative projects. So, when you identify a drain, before you try to block it, ask yourself what pillar or priority is being served by that creative cost. Activity 1 in this chapter is designed to help with this process.

Look for the Small Outflows

As you're considering your outflows, the big ones will be easiest to notice, but the small drains often do the most to put you in a depleted state. Do not underestimate the draining power of daily dishes and laundry. Finding and reducing small drains is a large part of the *Productivity* section of this book. When you fix something annoying in your physical space, you have reduced a source of depletion. When you create onramps to your creative projects, you've reduced a source of depletion.

Connect With Your Network

Communicating with your support network can be a critical element in helping you reduce outflows. It might look like sitting down with your household to redistribute some of the draining maintenance tasks of living. It might look like connecting with someone who carries similar burdens and struggles so you can vent emotions and help each other brainstorm solutions. If finances allow, it might look like hiring someone to take on tasks. (I dream someday of hiring house cleaning help!) Connections with others can have a creative cost, but those same connections can also give you solutions and inflows.

Put Boundaries Around Your Outflows

When an outflow is necessary, you may still want to put boundaries around it to control the rate of flow. My small business includes a lot of administrative work to produce, market, and ship physical products. This work is necessary, but it will use up all my available energy and time if I let it. I have a hard time cutting off admin work to switch to my creative projects, especially if the admin work feels unfinished. But just like water will flow and occupy any size space you give to it, some tasks in your life will fill all the space you allow them. You have to make conscious choices on your part to give those tasks boundaries and then keep the tasks inside them.

Coping With An Unchangeable Outflow

What if you know exactly what your drains are, but you can't stop them because they're attached to priorities, dreams, or goals you're unwilling to give up? What if you have health conditions, care work, or other life situations you can't change that deplete you on a daily basis?

These sorts of situations are challenging. I've lived a life *full* of care work and demands that constantly pulled me away and sidelined the creative projects I wanted to do. I spent years raising young children and now my husband has disabilities that require my help. I never wanted to eliminate caring for my husband or children even when that care drained my aquifers and left little energy for my creative projects. Sometimes you have very little control over your outflows because they're directly tied to priorities, identities, or people you're not willing to abandon. Sometimes the work needs doing, and you're the only one who cares enough or is able enough to do it.

If this describes you, see if you can redirect a small portion of your outflow toward increasing your inflows. Some of that effort should go toward your network of supportive relationships. Can you redistribute some of the care tasks among members of your household? Can you find resources, grants, or respite services in your larger community?

Choosing Expenditure

There are times when you need to go all-out on spending energy instead of reducing depletion. Sometimes you might need to overspend on energy to manage a crisis or hit a deadline. In these cases, you spend abundantly to get things done even though you know that the inflow isn't enough to cover it. I call this "borrowing energy from my future self." When I do it, I know that future me will have to pay the bill for this expenditure of energy. I have to plan time to replenish once the push is done.

The health of an ecosystem, like the Cascades, depends on times of flood and drought. The same is true of your personal aquifer. The fact that your flows are out of balance during a particular day, month, or year does not spell doom for you or your creative projects. You just need to pay attention so that you can balance over time.

Increasing the Inflows

Just like reducing depletion, increasing your inflows requires an understanding of what recharges you and fills you up. Hopefully, you've already identified some inflows; if not, Activity 1 below may help you identify them. I also offer the following methods of increasing inflows that work for many people:

The Fast Charge

When charging a portable device, some plugs deliver a fast charge in an hour, while others take many hours for the same amount of charge. You need to discover what in your life can provide a fast recharge. Some possibilities:

- Get your knees above your head, place a cold pack on your neck, and breathe deeply for ten minutes.

- Take a 15-minute walk, outdoors if possible.
- Do 10-20 minutes of meditation.
- Create a ritual around making and eating a specific snack or beverage.
- Take a 20-minute nap.
- Do a quick act of service for someone else. It can be small, like feeding a pet or offering others a snack.
- Listen to a "recharge" playlist.
- Make someone else laugh.
- Something else *you* thought up.

Training your mind and body to accept recharge may take practice. So, if something is working a little, but not as well as you'd like, give it a week or so to see if it becomes more effective with practice.

Take a Break

When people talk about rejuvenation, it is often in the context of taking a vacation. Vacations serve a very useful purpose in forcing you to break your routine. That forced break helps you shake out old patterns of thought, and trying new things can fill up your creative aquifers. The trouble with vacations, however, is they are rare. If you rely only on vacations for replenishment, you'll spend most of your life depleted. Try to build a life that you don't have to escape from to be happy.

Think about how to give yourself small breaks. For example, do you take a break during lunch hour, or do you use it to catch up on different work? Giving yourself small periods of time during the day whose only purpose is to replenish yourself will keep you healthier, happier, and more functional in all aspects of your life.

Get Outside the Box

One of the best ways to discover what fills up your reservoirs is to try new things. These aren't necessarily big bucket list items. Small, local, inexpensive outings are better because if they work, you can repeat them.

To find options, do an Internet search on "things to do in [location]." Did you have a memorable beverage when you were on a trip? Can you find it locally or replicate it? Are there free craft activities at your local museum? Does the community college or high school near you offer low-cost classes in a skill you've wanted to try? Consider volunteering your time to a non-profit, school, or other organization. It may seem odd to spend energy on others when you're trying to replenish yourself, but helping others is a brilliant way to gain new experiences and create inflow. Service is surprisingly replenishing. Get outside your usual round of tasks and habits. Pay attention to how the new experiences make you feel and whether you feel more abundant afterward. Even if the new experience is uncomfortable or unpleasant, you've still filled your brain with new material to draw from when creating.

Be Your Own Guest

Much of the advice around rejuvenation is framed as "self-care." Unfortunately, like many ideas in capitalist society, self-care often turns into a list of items to purchase. I find it more useful to think of it as self-parenting. If you were taking care of someone else, what would you advise them to do? Yes, have the ice cream and watch a movie, but then go to bed on time and go for a run tomorrow morning. Self-parenting is thinking ahead and doing tasks now that will benefit your future self later. Thinking ahead to build rejuvenation into your plans solves a lot of depletion. Do the dishes tonight even though you're tired because that gives you a better start on the day tomorrow.

I once watched a show about renovating vacation rentals. The expert spoke about making the rooms inviting for guests. You can do the same for your own homes and life, creating spaces and life patterns that welcome you into them. Be your own guest and build places you don't want to leave.

Prepare a fun respite for future you. If a bubble bath with candles and a book is your jam, use some of your task hours to scrub the tub, lay out the candles, and buy the book. That way when the appointed hour arrives, you just run the water and get in.

Do for yourself all the little things you would do if you were about to welcome a guest into your home.

Create a Mid-Day Replenishment

One of the hazards of organizing your life to maximize creative output is that sometimes you make the mistake of removing the joys that fill you up from the schedule. Many productivity experts tell you to stop "wasting time." They don't understand that this "wasted time" can be an essential inflow. Creative minds need rest, particularly if they are of the variety that is always "on." For some brains, the only way to switch off all the thinking is to dive into binge-watching TV or playing a video game. Be alert for when you're overdoing it, however. While six to eight hours of sleep is necessary for health, fifteen hours is a sign that something is wrong. Similarly, an hour or two of video games may be refreshing, but ten hours of video games has almost certainly passed the point of diminishing returns.

Have a Jellyfish Day

When you anticipate a large outflow of energy, plan ahead to give yourself time where you don't expect to accomplish much. The amount of time should match the amount of depletion. During this time, drift like a jellyfish on the current. You may bump into tasks and work on them, but don't plan them and don't try to fix yourself in place. You're drifting and relaxing, not exerting effort. I try to schedule a jellyfish day after I have a big expenditure of energy (like attending a conference or an event). My jellyfish days often include consuming sugar and watching a lot of movies.

Only six months after I walked through the drought parched Cascades, the weather shifted and rain came. Lots of rain. Instead of concern there wouldn't be enough water, the news was full of plans for flood management. Those floods restored the dried landscape of the cascades, so much that parts of the area were closed for safety reasons.

Abundance can cause as many problems as depletion if not planned for. Like Cascade Springs, my depleted year was followed by abundance. In my case, I could see how being overburdened laid the groundwork for the abundance to come. Because I was prepared, the abundance was a joy. You can build systems that buffer against floods and droughts once you understand your flows. This is more than simply preparing reserves against times of drought — you want to build a life that has space for abundance.

Activities

Replenishment Activity 1
Depletion Analysis

Purpose: To take a look at the daily tasks of a recent week and do a quick assessment of whether your depletion and replenishment are in balance.

First, write a quick sentence or two about how you feel about your life in the past week. Do you feel it depleted you or replenished you?

Next, review the tasks and appointments from the last week and whether you accomplished them or not. Feel free to use any calendars or written lists you may have. You could also start with the *Priorities List* you made in Chapter 3 or the *Mental Load* list you made in Chapter 7.

Write the tasks and appointments in one column. Then, make a second column, and there, write a plus sign for the items that were depleting and a minus sign for those that were replenishing. If a task was both, write both symbols. If you want more detail, you can give extra letters to items that were particularly depleting or replenishing.

Count the number of plusses and minuses. Were they out of balance this past week? Does the count match your general assessment of how the week went? If your summary assessment and your analysis count were significantly different, you may want to repeat this activity next week to see if you can improve your assessment skills.

Replenishment Activity 2
Pick an Experiment

Purpose: To try experiments to find some things that will provide you with replenishment.

Pick one of the activities below (or design your own based on your needs) and try it. When you are done, reflect on whether the experiment accomplished what you hoped. If you want, pick another activity and repeat.

- Outside the box. List five things you've always wanted to do but never have. If you can, pick small, local, and inexpensive outings. Over the next month, do at least three items from your list. Each time you return from one of these outings, sit down and write your thoughts about the activity. Also note if your next creative work session feels different.
- Be your own guest. Plan to prepare a fun respite for future you. This can be the bubble bath described earlier in this chapter or something else entirely. Whatever you pick, make sure you plan ahead and smooth out all the details so that your future self only has to enjoy. At the end of your respite, take some time to write and reflect on this experience. How did it work for you? Did the extra work to set up in advance seem worth it? Do you feel replenished? Do you have ideas for what to do differently with a future experiment at being your own guest?
- Small replenishments. Sit down and make a list of small things that bring you joy. They should be relatively inexpensive and simple things, like a freshly made bed, a snack you enjoy, or a book to read on your lunch break. Pick one of these small replenishments and decide how to deploy it in your life for the next two weeks. At the end of those two weeks sit down to write and reflect on the experience. Did the replenishment help you? Did it become another chore that adds to your mental load?
- The fast charge. Look at the list of possible fast charge activities earlier in this chapter. Select one to try as an experiment. Repeat on a regular schedule for the next week or two. Check if repetition and practice increase the benefit you get.

Productivity

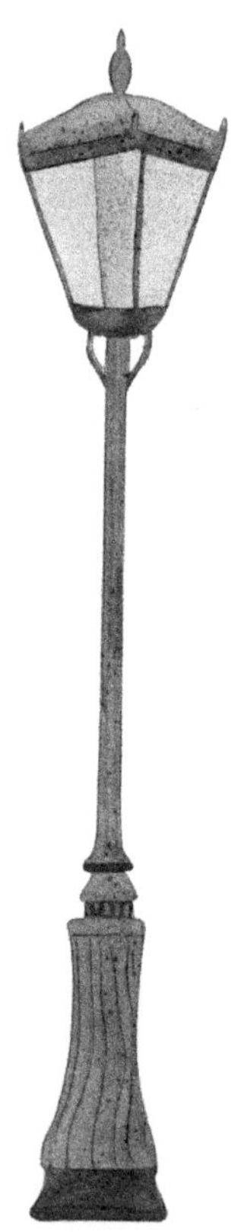

Chapter 10

Curating Your Commitments

In 2021, I found myself beset with calendar appointments and tasks. Much of the creative work I wanted to do was crowded out of existence. I tried to hurry and finish tasks to cross them off my list, but everywhere I turned I found more. I'd been trying to write a simple blog post and newsletter for days and kept trying to figure out what I could eliminate to give me more breathing room. I was frustrated and restless, so I got outside my box. I had to shove other tasks out of the way to make it happen, which made me anxious, but I masked up against COVID and took myself to a yoga class at my community fitness center. During class, I breathed. Literally. When class was over, I wrote the blog post and newsletter easily. I knocked several other tasks off my list as well. The effect was so profound I immediately put more yoga classes on my calendar.

The addition of this yoga class gave me new inflows and forced the rearrangement of my outflows in a way that decreased them. It also helped me align with priorities I had neglected, like tending to my physical health. It lightened my mental load by giving me an hour where I was excused from all of my tasks.

When you're struggling with your balance of life and creative work, sometimes the answer is addition, and others, subtraction.

YOUR CREATIVE WORK THRIVES WHEN YOU MATCH YOUR COMMITMENTS TO YOUR PRIORITIES AND ENSURE THAT YOUR SCHEDULE BALANCES ACTIVITY AND OPEN TIME.

Commitments mean more than calendar appointments. They are also food resource management (AKA grocery shopping), childcare, and elder care. They include the text chain you maintain with a friend group. They're anything you've agreed to do and anything you've assigned to yourself.

External Structure is Helpful

One reason adding the yoga class was so helpful was that it provided some external structure to my days. At the time I was self-employed and therefore completely in charge of my own schedule. This meant if I decided 8:00 am was my writing time, the only thing getting me out of bed was my decision and my willpower. In Chapter 7, *Managing Mental Load*, I discussed the difficulty of using willpower to hold things in place. Declaring a schedule and trying to hold yourself to it is a lot like holding a five-pound weight at full arm extension. At first, it is easy, but your arm quickly gets tired and begins to droop. If you rest your wrist on the back of a chair, you can hold that weight for much longer. Similarly, when you use external structure for your schedule, you reduce your willpower expenditure and ongoing effort.

I had to be at yoga at a specific time or I would miss class. Thus, my day divided into "before class" and "after class." Some of my daily tasks made sense to schedule beforehand and others, after. Sorting my tasks this way reduced my decision load. It also created some urgency about getting the "before class" tasks done.

As you consider your commitments, pay attention to which ones might provide you with the external structure you need. The structural value of that commitment must be weighed against the time spent on it and its creative cost.

Align Commitments with Priorities

One of my priorities is taking care of my health. At least, I say it is one of my priorities, but the truth is that I frequently skip health-related tasks. When I put yoga into my schedule, I was bringing a tiny piece of my life into better alignment with my priority. It also meant I could let go of my guilt for not exercising more. That guilt was small, but every bit of guilt I get rid of makes more space for my creative projects.

So, when looking at your commitments, you'll want to have your Priorities and Identities Lists handy. Each of your commitments should connect to or support of one of your priorities or identities.

Testing for Joy

Consider each of your commitments and whether it is a net benefit in your life or the lives of others. Don't neglect that second part. I have many commitments that don't bring me personal joy but bring happiness to someone I care about deeply. Their happiness does bring me joy, so in a roundabout way, the commitment is worth it.

One way to test your commitments is to pick a day or two and excuse yourself from your to-do list. This is not a vacation with planned activities outside your usual round of activities. Ideally, you don't leave your regular spaces. Instead, you ask yourself, "What do I want to do right now?" When you find the answer to that question, go and do it. When you finish the thing, ask the question again. Maybe you spend the day watching movies, or maybe you go out for ice cream. Maybe you dive into a house project that has been waiting on the back burner. Maybe you get the laundry done that's been bugging you for weeks.

Sometimes, when I try this experiment, I will discover that I accomplished most of the things that would usually have been on my list, but in a way that felt joyful and relaxed instead of regimented and stressed. The reconnection to my desire to accomplish those things is very useful. Other times, I find that I binge-watched a TV show because my brain and heart needed a period of rest and recuperation. Occasionally, I fill the day with creative projects. I like those days, because it indicates to me that my regular schedule is not depleting me. The natural state of human beings is to grow and create. If that is not happening, there is a source of depletion preventing you from flourishing.

Corralling Urgency

A life organization principle I learned from having a Franklin Planner in the 1990s is the difference between *important* and *urgent*. Important activities connect to your priorities and dreams. Urgent ones have a short timeline with consequences. A nearly-due report for work is urgent; spending time with your child is important. Urgency is real, but you can spend your life responding to urgency, shoving important priorities out of your days.

While running our creative business, my husband and I realized that if we didn't pre-plan and put the family vacation onto the calendar first, there would not be one. So, in November or December, I would plan a vacation for spring, make reservations, and put it on the calendar. Then, as everything else came up, it had to bend around the reality of that family commitment. When the trip arrived, it was never conveniently timed. We always had urgent things going on. Sometimes, we packed work to take along with us, but for that week, urgent tasks had to bend around family time, when, in so much of our lives, it was the other way around.

Putting important activities into the schedule first is one way of corralling urgency and giving it boundaries. You can also try the following strategies:

- **Reality check.** Check in with another person who knows the situation to determine whether something is as urgent as it feels.
- **Habitual urgency.** If a particular task always ends up as a near-crisis before it gets done, your system around that task is not working. It might be time to create a new system, engage help, or hand off that task to someone else.
- **Defined work times.** Tasks like email are constantly urgent. It can help to plan certain parts of the day to deal with them and other parts of the day where you excused yourself.

For example, try devoting two hours of your day to email management. Anything that doesn't get done in that time frame has to wait until tomorrow.

Excusing Commitments from Your Life

In deciding whether a commitment needs to be cut from your life, I invite you to ask yourself the following questions:

- Does it spark joy or make you happy?
- Does it maintain an identity or a priority?
- Does it provide structural support in your schedule?
- Does it move you toward a dream or a goal?
- If the answer to all the questions is no, then drop that commitment or find a way to reframe it so you can answer yes to at least one of these questions.

It is easy to say "Cut out that commitment," but often harder to accomplish. Particularly if the commitment involves other people who will be disappointed or upset by your decision to step away. A desire not to disappoint others can keep you stuck in situations that are not serving you. Sometimes serving others is more important than serving ourselves. If you can't cut a commitment, then reframe that commitment in your mind as a deliberate service you give. Thinking in terms of service may help the commitment connect to one of your identities or priorities.

Suppose you do decide you need to cut a commitment, even if others are disappointed. In that case, review the "Necessary Conversations to Reframe Relationships" section in Chapter 6, *The Boundaries You Need*. Make a plan to have a conversation and hold strong to your decision. Quitting gets a bad rap, but sometimes it is the right call.

Activities

Commitments Activity 1
Reality Check

Purpose: To double-check whether you can actually do all you've assigned to yourself in the time that you have available.

Sit down with your calendar and task lists for your busiest day in the coming week. List your tasks vertically in one column. In the second column write how much time you expect each task to take. (I recommend rounding to fifteen minutes for ease of math.) If the task or appointment requires travel time, include that time as part of the length of the task. Make sure you list any planned time for your creative projects. Next list any recreation or rest you intend to have and how much time you want to spend. Make sure you include sleep on your list.

Now add fifteen minutes of "transitional time" between each task or appointment. If a block of tasks is clumped together and you can move smoothly between them, you can leave out the transitional times for that block.

Add up all of the time amounts. If the total is more than 24 hours, you must adjust what you expect yourself to accomplish for that day. If most of your days are similarly overscheduled, you need to make conscious decisions about what to cancel or deprioritize.

Commitment Activity 2
Priorities and Commitments

Purpose: To compare your commitments to your priorities and ensure they match.

Take your *Priorities List* and compare it to your current schedule of commitments. You can do this by looking at your calendar and task lists, remembering your commitments, or by writing out your commitments as a list. If you want, write them side by side in columns or use separate notecards you can slide around.

Do all of your commitments connect to a priority? Are the commitments you have truly serving your priorities? Are there different commitments that would serve you better?

Commitment Activity 3
Project Assessment

Purpose: To connect projects to priorities and consider if your current set of commitments can be adjusted to support those projects better.

Pull out your *Creative Projects List* (from Chapter 1), your *Priorities List* (from Chapter 3), and your *Commitments List*, if you made one, from this chapter. Compare your commitments to your *Projects List* and your *Priorities List*. Then, sit down and free write answers to the following questions:

- Which projects are connected to your most important priorities?
- Are there commitments that directly support those projects?
- Can you add an activity or commitment to your schedule to support those projects?
- Can you subtract a commitment to make more room for the important projects?

Commitments Activity 4
Testing Your Commitments

Purpose: To experiment with how you would like to arrange your day when you're not constrained by your regular to-do lists.

Pick a day or two and excuse yourself from your to-do list as described in the section "Testing For Joy" in this chapter. Stay in your regular spaces, but when deciding what to do next, ask yourself, "What do I want to do right now?" When you answer that question, go and do that thing. When you finish, ask the question again.

At the end of the day, take some time to consider how your day was spent. Sit down and write answers to the following questions:

- Did your day go how you expected?
- How do you feel about how you used your time? Why do you feel that way?
- Do you feel more rested and relaxed or more stressed?
- Does this experience make you want to change anything about your current set of commitments?
- If your day was spent on things not in your usual round of commitments, why do you think that is? Do you need to give more regular space to the projects you want to be doing?
- Do you think your day helped you recover from depletion?
- Is there anything else that occurs to you?

Commitments Activity 5
Adding to Your Schedule

Purpose: To perform an experiment to measure the effect of adding a commitment to your schedule.

Pick a commitment to add to your schedule. You can choose a class, a coffee date with a friend, a ticket to an event, or something else. What you add doesn't have to be related to your creative projects. When you reach the day with the commitment in it, observe how having it on your calendar changes the shape of your day and your task organization. What became easier? Harder? Is the ease or challenge because the appointment is new, or do you think the ease or challenge will persist? Does adding something in the morning have a different effect than adding something in the afternoon?

This activity is most helpful if you repeat it and see how the appointment changes your patterns over time. How do different things you add and subtract have different effects?

Chapter 11

Your Physical Space

When my husband Howard took up cartooning "as a hobby," it became his full-time career very quickly. We stored all of his drawing supplies in a cardboard box that sat on the counter. When he set up to work, he'd take over the kitchen table. Then, after he was done, he'd stow everything back in the box. As cartooning became a fixture in our lives, he moved to a small, dedicated desk in the corner of our front room. Once it was an established source of income, we transformed the guest room into his office. Lately, because of long COVID fatigue, he's set up his supplies to work while reclining. My workspace has undergone similar transformations as the needs of my work and available resources change. Each of these work setups has had benefits and challenges. But through it all, we've learned that adjusting the physical space in which you work can help you get more creative projects done.

YOUR CREATIVE WORK THRIVES WHEN YOU TUNE YOUR PHYSICAL SPACES SO THEY SUPPORT THE PROJECTS YOU WANT TO DO.

Claiming a Space

Start by looking at what physical space is available to you. When you are ready to focus and create, where do you go to do so? You might have a dedicated office or studio space, or maybe you claim a corner of the couch in a shared living area. Many creative people rely on external spaces like coffee shops to get work done. Any of these (and a dozen other set-ups I haven't named) are completely viable options.

Depending on your life configuration, claiming a workspace may be complicated. My current workspace is distributed, which is a nice way to say that I don't have a space I can call my own. My bedroom is shared, my office is a windowless basement that people walk through, and my sunny writing corner is a very public space where people will randomly enter the room and start talking to me. I try to make the most of these available spaces, but it is a challenge.

In my ideal world, I would have a well-lit office with a window view of something scenic. This office would be mine alone, with a door I could use to shut out all the distractions of my household. In reality, I've put a little hydroponic garden next to the seat in my basement office. You may eventually want to dive into a large project to provide yourself with your imagined ideal working space but know also that having the perfect workspace is not a magic spell that will suddenly make you creative. Any workspace can be made to function with a little rearrangement.

A good workspace does not get in your way; it doesn't introduce barriers or frustrations into your workflow. An excellent workspace entices you to enter, but can't do the work for you. So, yes, pay attention to building a workspace, but don't worry about making it perfect. Get it arranged and then test it out by actually working. If you spend more time arranging the space than doing the work, you may have an avoidance issue. I'll talk about those in Chapter 14, *The Motivation Problem.*

Entering Your Workspace

Once you have your chosen workspace, you need a way to enter it. I emphasize entering and exiting your space because most human brains store thoughts locationally. You have probably experienced walking into a room, only to discover you don't remember what you came for. If you go back to the first room, you remember what you needed from the other room. It is as if in walking through a doorway you accidentally left the thought behind and have to return to retrieve it. This is called an "event boundary" or "the doorway effect" by scientists who study the phenomenon. And it is not just doorways that serve as event boundaries. You may have experienced the same thing when switching browser windows or scrolling back up through a social media feed to find a thought that got lost for a moment.

I had a fun experience of an event boundary recently. While watching a documentary, I was cooking pigs in blankets (Lit'l Smokies sausages wrapped in crescent roll dough). Several weeks later, someone else cooked the same dish, and I found myself thinking about the documentary I'd been watching. The thoughts of that documentary got stored in the same memory box as the smell of the food.

You can use this tendency of the human brain to your advantage. If you make event boundaries around your creative projects, when you need to step away and handle one of the other parts of your life, you can step back and find your creative thoughts there waiting for you. Scent is a powerful memory trigger. Clothing can also be surprisingly powerful. I know several writers who have "writing tiaras" they wear to help put themselves into writing mode. My husband, who works from home, can't really get into work mode until he has put on his shoes in the morning. What you choose is up to you. You only need to signal your brain it is time to work on your project.

Be creative about what you define as a workspace and how you define "entering" that space. During Howard's box-on-the-counter era of cartooning, he would "enter" his workspace by clearing one end of the kitchen table and opening up his box to pull items out. For a long time, my writing workspace was my laptop computer. I "entered" my workspace by sitting somewhere quiet and opening it up. I know writers with a single desk where they must do all of their administrative work, day job work, creative work, and recreational gaming. They create an "entry" by facing a different direction in the chair, changing room lighting, or putting on a special writing hat.

You also want to think about "exiting" when you're putting down your creative project. If you have time to consciously put things away, as Howard did with his cartooning box, then you have a ritual to help you disengage. Alternatively, if you have space, you could do the opposite. Instead of putting things away, deliberately lay out the tools and notes you plan to use next. When you re-enter your space for the next session you'll be able to pick up right where you left off.

Single-Use vs. Multi-Use

If space and finances allow, consider crafting a creative space that is separate from your work and play spaces. My distributed workspace assigns different locations to different kinds of creative projects: desktop computer for administrative and design work and laptop computer for writing and online socializing. These different tools allow me to enter a frame of mind while entering a space. However, a separate location is not always possible. Many of the spaces in my house must be multi-use. My kitchen table is routinely covered with bits of house projects, incoming packages, outgoing mail, and random accumulations. At the same time, I use that same table for sitting down to eat. Piles are frequently shuffled around. In an attempt to apply the "Be Your Own Guest" principle from Chapter 9, I frequently declare, "Nothing gets stacked on the table! It must always be clear so we can sit down and eat together." However, despite my declarations, the accumulation continues. This is because we have multiple uses for the table. To change that, I would have to create a separate "landing zone" for mail and a designated project space. Someday I hope to, but we don't currently have room, so the kitchen table remains a multi-use battle between clutter and dining.

If you have a single workspace used for multiple types of tasks, you may need to provide some a physical indicator to tell your mind and body this is *creative* time not *other stuff* time. It could be a placing a photo frame in your visual field with an image that reminds you of your creative goals. It could be a particular snack or a scented candle you light. Anything that helps your brain and body remember to switch modes even when you're physically in the same chair. If nothing else, you can do a mental reset by getting out of your chair and going for a walk or stretching. Physically step out of the role you were inhabiting and then re-enter the chair in your creative role.

The Sensory Experience

Once you have crafted a workspace to enter and exit, it is time to make sure the workspace supports the work you want to do. The space should support you, not distract or create obstacles. Tune in to the sensory experience of your space. Sit in your workspace as if you intend to start working, but instead look around. Observe the space using all your senses.

- **Sound.** Are there distracting noises? These noises may be subtle hums, or they might be household alerts like the buzzer on the dryer prompting you to get up and change the laundry. Changing the laundry is a good thing to do, but it can wait until creative time is over. What if you add a white noise machine, headphones, or speakers to control the audioscape of your space?
- **Touch.** What is the tactile experience of your space? Is your seat cushy or hard? Do you have a fuzzy blanket? Maybe fuzzy objects provide an unpleasant sensation for you and need to be evicted. Do you have a weighted blanket? Is there an encouraging plush animal you can pet when you're thinking? Is there a fidget toy handy so you can remain in the space while thinking? What tactile things can you change to make your workspace pleasant and non-distracting?
- **Smell.** What is the smell of your space? Are there food smells that will make you want to stop working and eat? Is there a hot drink or scented candle you can bring into the space to help anchor you there?
- **Taste.** You're probably not going to go around licking your workspace, but perhaps there is a snack that can accompany you into it.

- **Sight.** What are the visuals of your workspace? What do your eyes rest on when you look up from your work? If you can see your pile of guilt-inducing dirty laundry, then it becomes very easy to either spiral into how you fail at everything because you're staring at a huge pile of failure or to avoid your creative project by doing the laundry instead.

The simple process of this observation may give you a list of changes you'd like to make to your space. Or you can do the guided activity at the end of this chapter to reflect on those desired changes and make a plan to accomplish them.

Ergonomics

Another consideration for your creative workspace is convenience and ergonomics. Repetitive strain injuries accumulate, particularly as bodies get older. Consider whether the way that you sit, stand, and work is doing you harm. If you end up feeling stiff with an aching back after an hour in your space, look for a change that will allow you to work longer. Even if you don't consciously realize it, discomfort can pull you out of focus and send you off to the kitchen to look for snacks.

Are your creative supplies close to hand? If you're in the habit of using tape flags or scissors with your work, are they within easy reach of where you sit? If you have, like me, a distributed workspace, are those items within easy reach of all the places you sit and work? Every time you have to get up and look for supplies is a chance to get distracted. It is much better to have extra pairs of scissors than to waste time searching for the only pair you have. The same is true of pens, notebooks, etc. Does your workspace have a flat surface on which to set reference materials? Are your reference tools in easy reach of your workspace? If you are working with shared spaces and have only a small available space, you may not be able to set up an "ideal" space, but there are a surprising number of clever ways to take advantage of small spaces.

Conquering Clutter

Entire books have been written about how to organize your living and working spaces. Many of them have specific systems and instructions. I've included the names of several I like in the resources at the back of this book. However, any time you seek direction for how to organize, make sure that the process works with your brain and doesn't require you to develop new maintenance skills and habits. Many organizing systems add to mental load instead of reducing it. That is why they fail.

Here are a few organizational principles that have helped my household keep our home and workspaces usable:

- **Give everything a home**. The home for each item should be readily accessible and have enough space around it to allow your hand easy access. On top of only having one place for each thing, consider slightly anthropomorphizing your things (e.g., your keys are sad if they're not on their hook), which helps you put them away instead of putting them down.
- **Design for easy access.** Everything should be placed in a single row instead of stored behind or in front of other things. If you must move Thing One in order to put Thing Two away, then Thing Two will end up sitting on a random surface instead of in its home. Overstuffed drawers cause the same problem; it is too much work to put things away.
- **Distinguish supplies from resources.** *Supplies* are things you use often and need to be able to access at a moment's notice. *Resources* are things you only need occasionally, but want to own so you don't have to shop for them. Supplies should be front and center; resources can go in the backs of shelves or other less accessible storage spaces.
- **Maintain appropriate inventory.** When considering your supplies and resources, be honest about how much you need to store. Creative brains often spark with excitement over the potential of resources. Sometimes, however, you have to let go of that potential to make space for what you need.

- **Treasure empty space.** When your items are stored with empty space around them, you can see them to enjoy them, easily reach the supplies you need, and more easily put things away.
- **Cycle through the clutter.** It is completely normal and expected for projects to accumulate clutter while in process. The important principle is to include de-cluttering and clean-up as part of your creative cycle. Cleaning up your physical space between projects can help you clear away thoughts of the old project to start fresh.
- **Schedule clean-up time.** It might be as part of your regular creative time, or it might be as part of the time you set for household maintenance. Set a timer and clean up your workspace so it is ready for your next creative session. Ten minutes can do a lot when it happens regularly.
- **Pick a place to start.** When decluttering, look for one item whose storage location you know. Put that item away, then return and repeat. If leaving the clean up space will distract you, instead create piles or containers based on the items' homes. Once you accumulate a pile of "these things belong in the kitchen," you can transport the entire pile to the kitchen and deal with it there.
- **Clean from the corners.** This one comes straight from my mother. If you start in the middle of the room, it is tempting to let the corners stay messy. But if you start in the corners, you're less likely to leave the middle a big mess.

I could keep going. There are many ways to approach the organization of physical space, but for now, experiment with some of these activities.

Activities

Physical Space Activity 1
Observing Your Space

Purpose: To notice things in your workspace that may be causing you trouble and then perform an experiment to make changes to your space.

Sit in your workspace with note-taking tools. Make two columns, one labeled Positive and one Negative. Observe your space using all of your senses as described above and note down in the Positive column any of your sensory observations that assist in your creative projects, even if just feelings of happiness. In the Negative column, note down what is distracting or problematic.

Now, you're going to pick two things to change about your space. You can increase your positives (making your workspace more appealing) or decrease your negatives (making your workspace less distracting or problematic).

Once you've made your changes, write down your reaction to those changes. Repeat as often as you wish.

Physical Space Activity 2
Setting Event Boundaries

Purpose: To experiment with event boundaries as a way to help you enter your workspace and access your creative thoughts, then reflect on that experiment.

Considering the space you have available, pick one or two event boundaries or sensory triggers you want to teach your brain to associate with, "It is time to focus on creative projects now." Practice using that event boundary for a week or two to see whether it works as intended. Ideally, your change won't introduce extra steps between you and getting started working.

Write and reflect on whether the event boundary you created helped you.

Physical Space Activity 3
Ergonomics

Purpose: To potentially improve the ergonomics of your workspace.

At the end of your next creative session, take a moment to conduct a physical inventory of how your body feels. Do your wrists ache? Does your back feel stiff? Do some research into ergonomic solutions for the issues you uncover. Also, look up general ergonomic suggestions for your creative pursuits to see if they can be applied in your workspace. Choose one or more ergonomic improvements that fit your budget of effort and money. (Place a time limit on how much research you do, so you don't end up using "researching my workspace" as a way to avoid doing your creative projects.) Then, try out those changes for a week to see how they feel.

Chapter 12

Fragmentation of Creative Time

I once listened to a podcast where an established writer said he needed a solid block of four uninterrupted hours in order to make significant progress on his novel. One interruption would throw off his writing for the entire day. I laughed out loud, because I couldn't imagine having the luxury of four uninterrupted hours. At the time, I was juggling my jobs as primary caregiver for four young children, a growing role in the publishing business I share with my husband, and a desire to write books of my own. All my creative time was fractured and snatched from around the edges of everything else.

To be fair to the established writer (who is also a personal friend), there is some science around creative flow that shows an actual change in brain activity when a person is able to focus deep and long on a single task. I have (at a later stage in life when uninterrupted hours became possible for me) felt the creative joy of immersing myself in a project deeply only to emerge much later. I've come to understand that working in fragments of time and working in long stretches are both skills. There was an occasion during my fragmented years when I had an uninterrupted block of time, and I couldn't make proper use of it. My mind was too accustomed to interruption, so it interrupted itself. Similarly, the brain that is used to lengthy, deep focus has trouble making use of snatches of time. Which skill you should work to develop depends on the configuration of other parts of your life.

Deep focus vs. fragmented focus is like free diving vs. swimming on the surface. The surface swimmer doesn't get the compression and silence of the deep dive. However, the surface swimmer can grab a quick breath and get back to it, while the freediver has to spend energy coming up and then going all the way back down. Yet both swimmers can get across the entire body of water. How you swim doesn't matter as much as that you swim. You can even climb out of the water on a handy floating log to rest. What my established writer friend described in his four-hour writing blocks was akin to a scuba dive with special training, equipment, and probably a diving buddy or two. You can build your life structure to give you that. My friend certainly has. You can also build a structure, develop habits, and train your brain around much shorter periods of creative time.

> YOUR CREATIVE WORK THRIVES WHEN YOU PLAN AROUND AND BUILD SKILLS FOR THE BLOCKS OF TIME YOU HAVE AVAILABLE, WHETHER BIG OR SMALL.

Distraction Management

Whether your scheduled block of creative time is big or small, a core challenge is to keep distractions from stealing or fragmenting that time. It does not help that so much of modern technology and entertainment is deliberately designed to hack your brain. The human eye and brain alerts to changes in visuals. This is an ingrained survival trait. When something changes, humans are wired to check and see if a tiger is stalking them. Films, social media, and advertising are designed to push that alert button over and over again. They hack your attention to make money.

An unintended side effect of this attention hacking is that the frequent scene changes and attention grabbers train your mind to expect a constant flow of new information. You have to learn how to defend against these alert cycles. A good starting point is the notifications you receive from apps and programs on your electronic devices.

I have set my notifications so the only thing that can ping me is a human who deliberately requests my attention. Phone calls and text messages make my phone ping. My game, social media, and news apps do not. I still check those apps but when I decide to, not when an alert pulls my attention away from something else.

If you're accustomed to having instant notification of every social post by friends or of when your package is nine stops away, turning off these notifications may cause you some anxiety. But choosing when to engage with tech rather than letting tech claim your attention is an important boundary for defending your creative project time. Alert your social circle that you're experimenting with your notification settings, however — you don't want them to worry when it takes you longer to respond.

Even with notifications turned off, your tech encourages you to fill every spare moment with new information. With the Internet in your pocket, you never have to be bored. Except that boredom is the creative person's friend. When you're bored, your creative mind makes up stuff to fill the space. Learning to be comfortable with boredom helps fill your creative wells. Learning to be present in your current moment rather than distracting yourself will help you take advantage of your creative time later.

Useful Distraction

Some people have trouble focusing on a single thing at a time. I know of artists who listen to audiobooks or music while drawing to keep the word-focused portions of their brains occupied while they're creating visual art. Some people find it easier to listen to a lecture if they're also doing something kinesthetic like knitting or drawing. Some play a game on their phones while watching a show. If you possess one of these multi track brains, multi-tasking can be a way to maintain focus rather than interrupting it. I'll talk more about adapting for this sort of brain in Chapter 19, *Your Access Needs*. In the meantime, recognize that while you *can* train and build up your capacity for a single focus, it might be uphill work. You may be better served by intentionally pairing your focuses. A good pairing for your creative project will keep you in your workspace longer.

Claiming Time

You need to set aside time for your creative projects. This is important whether you're trying to claim a four-hour block or a fifteen-minute one. Make deliberate choices about what hours or minutes you are available for creative projects and what hours you're available for everything else. When you start setting these boundaries, be prepared for friction and resistance from people who are accustomed to being able to interrupt you. Use the relationship skills discussed in Chapter 6, *The Boundaries You Need*, to have conversations with the people in your life.

It might not just be other people who interrupt your project time. It might be *you* who interrupts you. Put some thought into how to prevent you from interrupting yourself. Perhaps you will need to deploy some tech tools to cut off your access to online distractions or games during your work time. There are a multitude of options for corralling yourself into your workspace.

Something Is Better than Nothing

No matter how little the amount of time you have available, you can put it to use. If you only have five minutes to scribble a note before moving onward with your day, scribble the note. Now you have a note which you didn't have before. If all you can do is look at your project and try to remember what you were doing, you're in a better position to continue your work than you were before. **Any progress is progress**. Let go of the idea that your progress must measure up to anything else. It is easy to become discouraged when you hear about the processes other creative people have established or the progress they've made.

Any process that lets you create is better than one that doesn't.

Do not worry if your process and systems don't look like those of other creative people you know or admire. Yes, listen when other creators talk about their process, but don't treat their word as gospel. If you think something they do will work for you, adapt it to your structure. If you try an idea out and it doesn't work, let it go.

Skill Building for Large Blocks of Time

To build structure and skills around large blocks of time, consider trying one of these ideas:

Collaborate with and Train Your Support Network

If you need uninterrupted blocks of time, the people who share your life need to be on board with giving you those chunks of time. They need to understand that a two-minute interruption in a two-hour block means you no longer have a two-hour block; you have two one-hour blocks. Deploy your skills from Chapter 6, *The Boundaries You Need*, and negotiate a time block experiment you think will work for everyone. Also, set clear signals for when you can be interrupted and when you need to be left alone. It can be anything from a closed door to a work hat that allows others to assess at a glance — without interrupting you — that you're doing focused work and should be left alone.

Learn to Dive Deep

One of the big challenges of the "long block of time" method is that the advent of social media, which is designed to interrupt your thoughts constantly, training your brain to seek constant stimulation and resist focusing deeply on your creative craft. If you want to make use of big blocks of time, you need to practice teaching your brain to use the time fully. You wouldn't sign up for a marathon and run it the next day without training. Uninterrupted time won't help you if you interrupt yourself. Look to Activity 4 later in this chapter for practice at thinking deep.

Skill Building for Small Blocks of Time

If you want to build structure and skills around small blocks of time, here are some ideas to help:

Segment your process

Some of your creative work takes place solely in your brain and can be done while handling other tasks. Other parts of your creative projects require you to be uninterrupted in your workspace. Do your best to use your uninterrupted time only for the tasks that require you to be uninterrupted. You can think about characters while watching your kids in the park. You can visualize art while driving to work. Then, when you sit down, you can make the thing you've been thinking about because the pre-thinking is done.

Catch thoughts on the fly

As you move through the world, practice catching stray thoughts about your creative projects. A method I like is to carry a notebook for jotting down ideas. The act of making the note tells your brain that stray thoughts about your creative projects are important and your brain should keep track of them. It also helps you cache the thought where it won't be lost. The thought is safe; you can return your attention to what else you were doing.

Visualize

I often picture my creative thoughts as inhabiting a cupboard. When I'm in writing mode, I open the cupboard doors wide and have access to all the project thoughts. At other times in my life, I tuck things neatly away, close the cupboard doors, and focus my attention on other portions of my life. I know a student who studied by using this sort of visualization. As he learned a piece of information, he visualized putting it into a specific cubby. Then, when test time came, he could look into the cubby and find the information. You can train your brain to hold and retrieve creative thoughts in this same way, allowing you to release and retrieve creative thoughts at will.

Set triggers

These could be based on the flow of your day such as "When the baby goes to sleep, I write for half an hour." Or they could be reminders of thoughts you had when you last put your project down. Those reminders could be plotting questions on sticky notes you place around your house, reminding you to think about the plot. Or they could be notes in your working file to remind you what you plan to do next. The key is to give yourself an easy grabbing point to start driving your project forward.

Smooth your speed bumps

Pay attention to the small speed bumps. If you have five minutes to work, but your workspace chair is buried in laundry, that will block you from using those five minutes. Figure out what causes a pile of laundry to land in your chair. Can you build a better process so laundry never lands in your work chair again? This is only one example of a speed bump, a tiny thing standing between you and the creative projects you want to do, preventing you from starting. Some fixes will be easy to implement right away. Others will have to go on a list for later. Still, even if you can't remove a speed bump completely, you can often find a way to smooth it out. Even just being consciously aware of a speed bump can help you get over it. There is a short-term creative cost to smoothing out the speed bumps, but the long-term gain is usually worth it.

Engage hyperfocus

Identify habits that help you open the doors of your creative cupboard and dive into your project. This could be entering your physical space, setting up a musical project playlist, or other environmental reminders. You can also challenge yourself. Instead of thinking, "Oh, I've only got fifteen minutes; that's too short to get started," reframe the thought as, "I've got fifteen minutes; how much can I get done in that time?"

Using Your Creative Time Wisely

Whether you have large blocks of time or small ones, it is possible to segment the time available within those blocks. Odds are good that your creative project requires you to spend time on research, business activities, or marketing. If you only have one hour of creative time per day and spend all of it on social media management, then something is out of balance. You need to think through what balance you want to have. Say you have an hour for creative work and you want to spend 50% on creating, 10% on supporting tasks, 20% on admin (like answering email), and 20% on marketing via social media. By knowing those percentages, you are empowered to do the math and divide your available time. Then, you can set timers to keep your various tasks in bounds. If your hour of creative time per day is distributed into three blocks of ten minutes and one block of thirty minutes, you can look at the creative tasks and pick which task receives which available block of time.

Activities

Fragmentation Activity 1
Practice Thinking Deep

Purpose: To practice single focus for a sustained time.

Pick a set amount of time — thirty minutes is a good starting point for many adults, but feel free to make it shorter. Set a timer and, for the allotted amount of time, deeply dedicate yourself to one activity, like a reading a book on paper, practicing piano, or meditation. Any time your brain wants to jump away and think about something else, gently bring it back to the task at hand. When your timer goes off, you're done.

Repeat the activity on a regular schedule (I suggest daily) for several weeks.

An alternate version is to practice single focus on the go. For example, take yourself on a walk and leave your podcast or music behind, or wait in line without pulling out a social media distraction.

After you've practiced for several weeks, sit down to write and reflect. Have you noticed changes in your ability to focus? Have your stress levels changed? Have you noticed any impact on your replenishment or depletion? Does this effort feel worth continuing or are you better off trying a different experiment?

Fragmentation Activity 2
Managing Your Notifications

Purpose: To tune your notifications and make conscious decisions about what is allowed to interrupt you and what needs to wait.

Sit down with your most used devices (probably your phone, tablet, or computer) and open up the notification settings. For each app on the device, decide whether it is allowed to send you push notifications that chime or vibrate. Change your settings and choose the length of time to keep the changed settings. I recommend a week or longer to help you get over the natural anxiety that happens when your brain doesn't get the constant notifications it is accustomed to.

At the end of your week, write and reflect. Did the lack of notifications cause problems for you? Have your stress levels changed? If your stress is higher, is that because of actual problems caused by the lack of notifications or because your brain is still accustomed to updates and struggling with waiting for them? Do you want to adjust your experiment?

Fragmentation Activity 3
Practice Using Small Bits of Time

Purpose: To demonstrate how small amounts of time can be useful and how small progress still counts.

Set a timer for just five or ten minutes. See how much you can get done on your current creative project in that time. If you have trouble making yourself do this, pick a random writing or visual prompt that is not your main project. The key is to demonstrate to yourself how useful a mere five or ten minutes can be. How many words can you get down on paper in that time? How much of a page can you fill? How many rows can you crochet? Suppose you can do this same five or ten minute three times a day. Do the math on the words written, pictures drawn, or rows created. It all adds up.

Fragmentation Activity 4
Smoothing Speed Bumps

Purpose: To identify speed bumps in your creative process and make a plan for smoothing them out.

Sit down in your workspace with note-taking tools. Pay attention as you enter your space, do your work, finish your work, and exit. Write down all the speed bumps you identify.

Pick three speed bumps that are the most likely to disrupt your creative projects. Write down how you can smooth them out. Does your reference shelf need to be moved into easy reach so you don't have to get out of your chair to check something? Do you need a dedicated blanket folded up and waiting for the moments when you feel cold? Do you need to put the folders for your creative projects front and center on your computer desktop so you don't have to go looking for them?

Make a plan for smoothing out at least one speed bump. List items you might need to buy, actions you need to take, or any tasks necessary to smooth the bump. Set reminders about these things.

Fragmentation Activity 5
The Pie Chart

Purpose: To define how much of your creative time should be spent on admin vs creative work and experiment with applying the decision.

Write a list of your creative tasks, including both your creative projects and the supportive, administrative, and marketing tasks related to it. What percentage of your available creative time do you want to spend on each of these tasks? If it helps, draw a circle and represent the percentages visually as a pie. You can also skip the list writing and talk this through (out loud) with a sympathetic listener.

Once you decide on your percentages, try applying them using reminder tools to ensure each activity stays in bounds. Then, reflect on how well it worked for you or whether the division of your creative session broke some of your processes.

Chapter 13

Time Scheduling and Project Management

I once saw a professional juggling performance while visiting my local zoo. The pair of jugglers laughed, danced, and told jokes, all while keeping a variety of objects whirling through the air. It was mesmerizing. I could not see how so few hands could constantly catch and release so many objects without fail. I returned home and told my husband Howard about the jugglers. "This is what my life is like, more things to keep control of than I have available time, energy, or hands. Sometimes, the only solution is to fling the balls in the air and hope to have a hand free when they come back down." Howard nodded and then very wisely pointed out that jugglers fling their balls as a deliberate performance. In real life, if you really want to not to drop any balls, you need a bag, not juggling lessons — especially since, as noted in Chapter 3, *Priorities*, some balls are rubber while others are glass.

Since that realization, I've sought ways *not* to be juggling. I've used different digital and physical tools to help me track and manage projects, everything from project tracking software to paper planners to simple notebooks. My tools and systems change depending on my projects and other life responsibilities.

YOUR CREATIVE WORK THRIVES WHEN YOU HAVE A PROJECT MANAGEMENT SYSTEM TO TRACK ALL ASPECTS OF YOUR LIFE, INCLUDING YOUR CREATIVE PROJECTS

Tracking Tasks

Learning alternate ways of managing tasks is particularly important if your brain or body is not well suited for juggling. My brain naturally tracks tasks and deadlines. Task juggling works for me because I can stare into the distance and see all the balls with my peripheral vision. My husband Howard's brain does not track things. He focuses on the ball he's about to catch and ignores all the others until they are in his hands. These differences create advantages and challenges. I love my ability to track, but I often get tangled up worrying about things that don't need to be managed for months. In contrast, Howard is frequently surprised by deadlines that sneak up on him, but when the time comes to work, he can quickly put aside everything except the task at hand. The systems Howard uses to track and manage are different from mine.

Project Management Strategies

The array of possible project management tools is large. Exploring it all in detail would take the remainder of this book. Instead, I shall trust your ability to research readily available tools, and I will focus on organizational strategies that have been helpful to our projects and can be applied to the tools you choose. The time scheduling and project management structure you develop for your creative projects should play to your strengths, whether that means finding the right bag or developing skill in juggling.

Color Coding

Color catches your eye and helps you focus. Monochrome makes all of the information seem of equal weight. You can use color to draw your eyes to important project tasks or deadlines. On a calendar with multiple projects, I assign each project a different color so I can easily track appointments and tasks related to it. I have done this with the family calendar as well, assigning each kid a color. Howard and I share a project spreadsheet as well, with incomplete tasks marked in red and completed ones in green. I use sticker tabs in my notebook, one color to mark ideas for books or blog posts, another color for story ideas, and a third for poem fragments. The colored tabs stick out from the pages and help me find what I'm looking for later.

Keep it simple when first deploying color coding, and only use one color code per tracking system. If you're using red and green to mark complete / not complete, red and green should not be used as primary colors for a project on the same calendar.

Project Cupboard

Since my brain does not naturally put aside thinking about one project when I engage with another, I have developed strategies to help me focus on one task instead of all the tasks. As I previously mentioned, I have a mental cupboard where I store thoughts about my projects. In there, I imagine myself putting my fiction thoughts when I'm supposed to work on nonfiction. I also have physical spaces where I store my projects. I have drawers and boxes for my various hobbies so the tools for sewing are separate from the tools for calligraphy.

Lately, I've created separate digital spaces for projects. I open a separate browser window for each of my freelance projects. This allows me to group all the tabs for a project into a single window. Then, I can minimize that window while working on something else. Staring at the tabs for a freelance job while I am trying to research a book tugs my thoughts away from the research at hand and into the freelance work instead.

When I put things away for a project, I organize them so that when I'm ready to return to the project, I can quickly re-orient around what I need to do next. If I have a stray thought for one of the projects I'm not focused on today, I quickly make a note (either digital or physical, text or voice) and stow it in a place where I'll find it when I re-open that cupboard. Making the note allows my mind to let go of the idea instead of trying to hold it.

Boomeranging

Related to the project cupboard is the need to be able to set a task for myself to accomplish next month but make it vanish from sight and mind until then. There are multiple tools for accomplishing this; my current favorite is to send myself an email and then snooze that email until the relevant day. I fling the memory of the task out into the future, trusting it will reappear in my inbox later.

Returning to Zero

Howard has no trouble ignoring his other projects for the one at hand, but he struggles greatly with distractions, following tangents and side quests. So, we create a home base, or zero position. Imagine that the task is to clean up your bedroom. As you're cleaning, you create piles of items to put away in other spaces. Stack these piles on the bed, which becomes "zero." When you carry a pile to put it away in another location, instead of getting distracted by all the other tasks, you remember you need to return to zero. That way, you return to the bed where the piles remind you what you were doing. If you check in with zero, you can better remember what you're supposed to do next. For most of the projects Howard and I share, zero position is a project spreadsheet listing all the tasks that need to be done. The shared spreadsheet is useful for me and essential for Howard.

Task Clumping

I've discussed task clumping previously, but it is so useful, I'm covering it again in this context. If you can connect tasks together, they become one juggling ball instead of two. This is commonly seen in such tasks as a "bedtime routine" or "skincare routine." The routine contains many separate steps, but in your brain and on your schedule you treat them like a single item, making it easier to plan. I often clump my tasks by assigning them to days. Monday is grocery day. Since I'm already in the car and out of my house, I clump other errands onto that day, too. If I simplify the errands so they don't require much thinking, then I can use errand time to pre-think what I want to write next. In contrast, Tuesday is laundry day, which pins me to the house with small tasks while waiting for laundry machines to cycle. I can alternate switching loads with other household chores or use the interim moments to challenge myself to write some words before the load is done. For you, if "laundry day" means a trip to a laundromat, perhaps you can carry a portion of your creative project with you.

Task clumping creates structure, whether or not you assign the clumps to specific days. A large, fixed clump of tasks forces other appointments or tasks to bend around it. When my kids were little, the need for a specific bedtime routine affected decisions I made all day long. This was sometimes frustrating, but it also gave me structure. When my kids were older, and I no longer had school schedules and bedtimes to build around, I tethered my schedule and task clumping to wake-up times and meal-times instead of to specific hours on the clock. If I clumped writing time to be "after breakfast," it didn't matter if "breakfast" happened at 8:00 am or noon: I knew how to flow from breakfast into my creative projects. This method of task clumping can be particularly useful for people who tend to become untethered from regular waking and sleeping times or whose schedules drift free from the clocks.

Checkpoints for Order-Dependent Tasks

One of the challenges for Howard is keeping track of where he is supposed to be in a project to finish it on time. To combat this, we create checkpoints. For a book project, we have checkpoints like "draft complete," "edit complete," and "send to printer." Set your checkpoints where they're useful. You could easily have a checkpoint of "per chapter written" or another measure that makes sense for your project. Put those checkpoints on the calendar by counting backward from your final deadline. If I want to send my book to the printer on October 1, then I need to complete the final edit by September 25. I probably need a month for the edit, and the editor needs a month to send me notes, so I need to have draft completed by July 25.

Because Howard's brain only pays attention to the one checkpoint right in front of him, he benefits from having daily or weekly checkpoints instead of ones that are months apart. For Howard we break down "draft" or "edit" into daily or weekly chunks. This is why setting daily word count goals can be very effective for some writers.

Checkpoints can help you with your project. Once you pick your checkpoints, set reminders or a system to help you track them. You'll also probably want to link your checkpoints to the zero position for the project.

Important note: missing a checkpoint is a moment for evaluation and recalibration, not shame. Since you missed the checkpoint, something in your creative plan isn't working as you intended. Were there unexpected crises? Did you mis-estimate the amount of work? Are you struggling with focus or avoidance? Skip spending energy on shame and instead treat your checkpoint result as data for your next experiment in productivity.

Another important note: if your creative project is collaborative, you may discover that some checkpoints get missed because of your collaborator, not you. If possible, build extra schedule time to give you and your collaborator space to be human. The complexities of working with a collaborator are outside the scope of this book, but a review of Chapter 5, *The Community You Need*, and Chapter 6, *The Boundaries You Need*, could be useful.

The System for You

I've just spent a lot of words telling you about systems that work for me. It is fine if your system looks nothing like mine. Any system that lets you track is better than one that doesn't. Your tools and processes should be personalized to you.

Activities

Project Management Activity 1
Tool Shopping

Purpose: To find tools to help you track your projects and experiment with them.

Find a person whose tracking system or work process is similar to yours. If you have a friend or family member who fits this bill, great! If not, look around at the social media of other creators. Learn more about how they track projects, either by observation or asking questions. Be mindful, however — research into how to track projects is a huge potential rabbit hole, and you could spend weeks or years seeking the perfect system (spoiler: there isn't one). Give yourself one week or less to pick something to try, whether it is an app, a notebook, or a corkboard with string. Try this project tracking system for a set amount of time. Depending on your project and life, your trial period might be a week, or it might be a month. You're performing an experiment to see if this system changes your ability to manage your projects.

The next three activities are strategies you can apply to this system.

Project Management Activity 2
Creating a Project Cupboard

Purpose: To create a physical or digital home for your project.

Create a physical or digital home for each project that is separate from your other projects. Some systems have separate project spaces built into them, giving you different "pages" or "boards" for each project you track. Other systems don't have this baked in, and you'll have to figure out how to do so. You might collect all your notes and pieces in your physical space into a box, binder, or drawer. If you're short on physical space, you can visualize the space you wish you had for this project. Then, when you're ready to engage with the project, close your eyes and visualize yourself entering that imaginary space, opening the cupboards, and setting up work.

Project Management Activity 3
Finding Your Zero Position

Purpose: To practice using the zero position technique to see if it is helpful.

Choose a zero position for your project. This is the place you will start from when you're ready to begin working. It might be a digital project board, a spreadsheet, or a physical desk. Any time you finish a task or a section of your project, return to zero and evaluate what comes next before launching into another task. If hyperfocus and flow are an important part of your productivity, it is fine to clump multiple tasks that flow together and complete all of them before returning to zero. But the practice of returning to zero will help you regulate so you don't over-extend one day and find work impossible the next.

Project Management Activity 4
Setting Your Checkpoints

Purpose: To set up project checkpoints for one of your projects to see if they're useful.

Use the process outlined in the "Checkpoints for Order-Dependent Tasks" section in this chapter to create checkpoints for your project. Make sure you have several checkpoints that fit inside the length of time you've set for your experiment along with a specific tracking system. You need to see how checkpoints work with your current system experiment. Notice if checkpoints you create for yourself work well or if you need external accountability and deadlines. Are you more likely to make your wordcount if you only have an hour at the library? Or is the looming library departure preventing you from getting started?

Chapter 14

The Motivation Problem

While parenting four young children, I was repeatedly faced with the challenge of motivating them to do chores they didn't want to do. I made many motivational charts, job wheels, and reward systems. Chores got done, but it was *me* creating a motivational structure for them according to *my* agenda. Once my kids hit their teenage years, the problem changed shape. To claim adulthood, they had to learn how to set their own agenda and motivate themselves. Several of them found this transition very difficult. They wanted to do tasks but struggled to make them actually happen. In trying to help them, I did a lot of thinking about motivation.

During this period, my struggling teenagers and I had many conversations about what they wanted and why they weren't doing it. Those conversations illuminated some fundamental differences in brain wiring between me and my children. Where I could implement a solo fitness plan, my kid required a workout buddy. Where I needed to set emotion aside to get tasks done, another kid needed to be in their feelings to make projects happen. I began to see motivation like an electrical circuit. You can build the most amazing gizmo, but the gizmo will remain inert until you line up all the wires with the power source. When the motivating force is connected, electricity flows, and everything starts moving.

YOUR CREATIVE WORK THRIVES WHEN YOU LEARN WHAT MOTIVATES YOU AND YOU PLAN YOUR LIFE TO CONNECT TO THAT NATURAL MOTIVATION.

The best place to start is by understanding your natural motivational modes. All these modes exist on a spectrum. I describe them in a binary this-or-that way, but you may discover you recognize aspects of multiple motivational modes in yourself. If you do, your self-assessment is correct — you are a complex being who defies simple labels. In addition, your motivations will change depending on your situation. I'll get into more detail about this in the troubleshooting section of this chapter. For now, these descriptions of motivational types and motivational tools should be a launching point for you to find ways to connect your motivational circuits so you can get moving.

Types of Motivation

Internal vs. External Accountability

I am a person who can simply assign myself tasks and then do them. However, one of my kids needs something outside himself to hold him accountable for the task. I can implement a solo fitness program, but my kid needs a workout buddy. Neither way of being is better; they just require different self-management techniques.

Curiosity-Driven vs. Results-Driven

Some people are motivated by completion or results. Others are motivated by curiosity rather than completion. School and most workplaces are set up to reward results. You are pushed to focus on getting projects done. If you're motivated by results, then most of society is designed for you. If you're motivated by curiosity, then you may face challenges in trying to get things done. The curiosity-motivated person picks up projects because something interests them and then drops those projects when the curiosity is satisfied. Twitter user @mykola beautifully encapsulates this idea in a thread posted June 6, 2023 (used with permission):

> *Your projects are your way of asking the universe a question, and then digging and digging and digging until*

the universe answers. You are motivated by curiosity, and that is a blessed gift, not a source of shame. Your unfinished work is the testament to your growth. Those aren't abandoned projects — those are the remaining scaffolds from the space ships that they launched. It was never about finishing the thing.

The accumulation of abandoned scaffolds can feel like failure because the world at large is results-focused. If you're curiosity-motivated, you need to find ways to complete projects even after the question or interest has been answered. I offer some ideas in the tools and troubleshooting sections in this chapter.

If you're motivated by results, be sure you remember to invest in the process rather than just rushing ahead to the finish. Again, neither of these ways of connecting your motivational circuits is right or wrong. They just require different approaches to make the projects happen.

Emotion vs. Dispassion

Some people can only connect their motivational circuits when they are fully connected to their emotional state. Others need to put emotions aside to get stuff done. If you are emotionally motivated, you probably have specific emotions that have the strongest connection for you. You might thrive on anger for your creations, or you might be drawn onward by hope and love. No matter what the emotion is, it functions as the live wire for the circuit. If you're dispassionate, then emotion interferes with connecting the circuit, much like static in a phone line can interfere with communication. The dispassionate person needs to spend energy processing emotions and setting them aside before focusing on creative projects.

Compliance vs. Noncompliance

Some people are driven forward by a strong need to connect and fit in with others. Others are driven by a need to be different or stand out. You'll probably experience both of these drives at some point. If you're motivated by compliance, this amplifies the usefulness of accountability partners and work dates. Your desire to fit in will get you moving. If you're motivated by noncompliance, you may need someone you can prove wrong or some "rule" you're deliberately trying to break with your project.

Troubleshooting Motivation

Avoidance and Resistance

As I tried to get my kids to do chores (like putting away their own laundry), they frequently would agree, but then I would discover them instead in the kitchen eating chips. I'd send them to do their chores again, only to find them reading a book. One day, I aimed one kid at the laundry five times in ninety minutes, and all five times they were distracted. It was like the laundry basket had an invisible forcefield pushing the kid away. I pointed this out; we talked about it, laughed together, and I once more attempted to point them at the laundry. Again, they deflected off the task by chattering at me about how they were avoiding it.

This sort of avoidance happens to everyone, usually on a subconscious level. In my house, we call it "the impossible task." Usually, the task could be accomplished in only a few minutes and isn't all that complicated, and yet is avoided for reasons you struggle to articulate. This sort of avoidance is not laziness. The amount of work that goes into avoiding is far more than the work necessary to do the thing. If you were lazy, you'd take the easier path. Something else is going on.

If you find yourself avoiding tasks, particularly ones related to your creative projects, you might be subconsciously protecting yourself from harm. You have a portion of your brain, the limbic brain (often called the lizard brain), whose sole job is to keep you safe. It does not distinguish between leopards and literary critics. It just pays attention, and if you approach something it thinks might be a threat, it will make you shy away from that threat. It does so wordlessly and on a very subconscious level, which is how, like my kid, you are suddenly interested in cleaning baseboards instead of working on your creative projects. Your limbic brain hijacked and redirected your attention onto something safe instead of something risky.

The "harm" you're trying to avoid may not be logically harmful. It might simply be boredom. Avoidance of boredom is particularly likely to strike if you're curiosity motivated. The assigned task doesn't hold your interest, so your brain seeks something that does. (This was absolutely the case with my kid and the laundry.)

Another way avoidance shows up is as negative self-talk. You attempt to work on your project, and your head fills with thoughts about the value of your project and whether you have the skills to make it happen. You might worry about the emotions you must unpack while creating the project. Or you worry about how your work will be received. Fear of rejection and critique, even in the far future, can stop you from doing your work today.

No matter the source of your avoidance, the first step to conquering it is to recognize that you're avoiding. Sometimes the recognition is enough to banish it and let you do the work. Other times you have to figure out the deep *why* of your avoidance. Telling yourself to "just get over it" and trying to willpower through avoidance is not a good long-term strategy. Instead, you have to find what you're afraid of and address it. I talk a lot more about self-doubt and fear in Chapter 18, *Cultivating Confidence*.

Anxiety as Motivation

If you are in the habit of procrastinating and then scrambling to get your projects done right before the wire, then the thing you're using to motivate yourself is anxiety. You're using fight-or-flight adrenaline to fuel your creative projects. This can be extremely effective, and you can get away with doing it for quite a long time; I've known people who've worked this way for decades. Unfortunately, it is hard on your body, and eventually the bill will come due. You will get sick or experience burnout. Anxiety as motivation is not a good long-term strategy for a sustainable creative life.

Learning from Other Toolboxes

I am internally motivated, results-driven, and deadline anxious. In 2020, a pandemic shut down the world and broke most of my motivational mechanisms. For months on end, I was unable to accomplish any creative projects. There are lots of reasons for that, many of which I discuss in Chapter 22, Grief is a Creative Process. The lack of clear results and deadlines broke my motivational structure. To get myself moving again I had to connect with curiosity as a motivation. Curiosity tools weren't impossible for me to use; they were just unfamiliar. However, these tools became increasingly useful as I gained skill with them.

When the world returned to a more familiar configuration in mid-2022, I welcomed the return of many of my former motivational strategies but also retained the skills I learned from using different tools.

The Connected Circuit Doesn't Work

Sometimes motivation is not the problem. No amount of current can get your projects moving if the gears are seized up. Other chapters in this book are designed to help you with that:

- You might not be moving because you're tired. (Chapter 9, *Depletion and Replenishment*)
- You might not be moving because your physical space is impeding you. (Chapter 11, *Your Physical Space*)
- You might not be moving because your sense of urgency is focused on other tasks. (Chapter 3, *Priorities*)

Connecting your motivational circuit and figuring out where you're jammed up can really help to get you moving again.

Activities

Motivation Activity 1
Identifying Your Modes

Purpose: To explore which motivational modes you use.

When considering which motivational modes come naturally to you, one of the best diagnostics is your gut instinct. Set a timer for about ten minutes and write about each motivational mode. Do you think it describes how you interact with the world? Which motivational modes describe you and your creative process?

If, at the end of writing, you're still not clear on which motivational modes you use, you can try one or more of the following activities to help figure it out:

- Ask someone close to you to read the descriptions of the motivational modes and then ask them which modes they see in you.
- Take Rubin's Tendencies Quiz, found on her website, gretchenrubin.com. She addresses internal vs. external accountability as well as compliance vs. non-compliance. Her terminology is somewhat different than mine.
- Evaluate the state of your projects. If you have lots of unfinished projects or hobbies you've dropped, that suggests you are, at least partially, curiosity-driven.
- If you have projects "go dead" after a time and you can't seem to care about them anymore (especially if you were previously in love with them), you might be emotionally-driven.
- If you push yourself to get a task done because crossing it off the list makes you happy, you might be results-driven.
- If you need to calm down and settle your mind before you work on creative projects, that suggests you're dispassionate.
- If you've ever created a project because someone told you it couldn't be done, you might be non-compliant.
- If you get things done because you don't want to upset or disappoint others, you might be compliance-driven.

Motivation Activity 2
Identifying Avoidance

Purpose: To see if there is a common theme in the types of tasks you tend to avoid so you can strategize on how to tackle them.

On a sheet of paper, create seven columns, one for each day of the week. At the beginning of your first day, write down the tasks you need to accomplish that day. At the end of your day, move forward any tasks you didn't complete onto the next day. Then, add any new tasks assigned for the next day. If you already have a system that includes this sort of task tracking, you can use your existing record to move forward with this activity.

When you have completed a week of record keeping, look at the types of tasks that routinely got pushed off onto the next day. How are they similar? Are they routine? Do they require decisions? Do they require social interaction, like making a phone call? You might want to run the analysis described in Activity 1 in Chapter 7, *Managing Mental Load.* Once you see the patterns in what you avoid, you can do some experiments with the tools in Chapter 15, *Managing Your Motion*, to see if they help you get tasks done.

Please be aware that this activity of making lists and tracking may be enough to change your behavior around getting tasks done. (New lists are a way to create challenge and interest for curiosity-motivated brains.) In this case, you may need to make this list from memory rather than from daily tracking.

Motivation Activity 3
Learning New Tools

Purpose: To interact with others as a way of investigating additional tools you can use.

Identify a person in your life who appears to be motivated and regularly on-task. See if they'll sit down with you either over lunch, a call, or via email so you can ask them questions. It may help to frame this as an interview where you say something like,

"I'm interviewing people to find out how they stay motivated and keep themselves on track."

Ask this person questions you've written down in advance. These might be a good starting place:

- Where does your motivation come from?
- How do you get yourself moving on a tired day?

Notice that the questions are open-ended rather than soliciting simple yes/no answers. As the person responds, take notes. Then, ask any follow-up questions that occur to you. Be curious. This not the moment to evaluate what will or won't work for you. You're collecting information, not judging this person's process.

If you have time and energy, performing the same sort of interview with additional people will give you more viewpoints.

After the interviews, consider the following questions:

- What motivational modes do these people seem to use?
- Do you have the same ones or different ones?
- Which of their tools and processes feel like they might help you?
- What experiment can you perform to try out one or more of their tools?

Chapter 15

Managing Your Motion

When I was growing up, Lego had an electric car set that our family built. We carefully constructed everything, connected the wires, and added the battery. Then we turned it on. It didn't move even though we could hear a slight hum from the motor. When I reached out a finger and tapped the car, that little push helped get it moving, and it rolled along just fine. It needed an extra nudge to overcome inertia. The car was not great at stopping by itself or turning either (it wasn't a great toy). For each change in motion, we had to give it a push.

In the last chapter, I talked about making sure you have everything connected so that motivation can move you. This chapter is about the extra nudge needed to start moving, turn, or stop.

YOUR CREATIVE WORK THRIVES WHEN YOU DEVELOP SKILLS AND TECHNIQUES TO HELP YOU MANAGE YOUR MOTION.

On-Ramps and Off-Ramps

One way to make getting started easier is to set up an on-ramp for your next creative session as you wind down your current session. This might look like notes dropped into your document, sticky notes on your desk, or materials laid out to be used. As you finish one task, set up the next task so that sliding into it is easy. A nice bonus is that setting up also serves as an off-ramp. Off-ramps let your brain switch modes away from your creative projects.

Managing Wait Mode

Another challenge to forward motion is wait mode. Wait mode is when you feel like you can't get started because you have an appointment later in the day, even if the appointment is five hours away and you clearly have time to get something done. I've experienced days-long wait modes before a big trip or hours-long ones before a phone call. Wait mode is an anxiety response. It is the fear that when the moment comes, you won't be ready. This fear gets compounded if you are prone to time blindness or often lose track of time. When you have many life experiences and memories of missed appointments you become afraid of missing the one ahead of you.

If you know you are prone to wait mode, tune your commitments with that in mind. You might be better served with a 7:00 am class instead of a 1:00 pm class if the latter will cause you to spend your morning in wait mode instead of getting tasks done. (Balance this against your natural early bird or night owl tendencies.)

One of the biggest tools for managing wait mode is recognizing when you have dropped into it. Sometimes, naming it "wait mode" is enough to bump you out and get stuff done. Alternatively, you can lean into wait mode and use the waiting time for rest and replenishment.

Task Transitions

One of the features of multi-focused, easily distracted brains is that they often have a hyperfocus mode. You have probably experienced this sort of hyperfocus at one point or another. It is when you look up and realize you've been working for hours though it only felt like minutes. Engaging hyperfocus can be great for project progress but can mean missed appointments, disrupted scheduling, and other challenges.

Even without fully engaged hyperfocus, some people struggle to transition between tasks. The practice of setting up off-ramps and on-ramps can help with this, as can setting multiple alarms. You might need to set a "prepare to stop" alarm and then a "time to stop now" alarm (and a "no, really, you have to stop now" alarm), while other people may manage with just a single alarm.

Sometimes, the struggle with transition is based on a lifetime of experience. You know that if you transition away from your current task, you will lose track of it or forget to come back and complete it. This fear is compounded when the "task" is your creative project. Trust that you are an abundant fountain of amazing thoughts and that the important cool thoughts will return. You can also develop off-ramps or systems to help you pick up where you left off.

If your brain is one that struggles with transitioning between tasks, you can get better with practice. I recommend looking up ADHD and autism resources for practicing transitions. These groups have abundantly useful toolboxes that can help anyone, regardless of diagnosis.

Reviving an Idle Project

When a project or creative practice has lain idle for an extended period of time, you may need an extra nudge to get moving on it. Start by collecting the pieces of your project into one place. Sometimes, just the act of review will spark the excitement that got you moving on the project in the first place. If you open an idle project and it feels dead and uninteresting, you may have shifted life priorities away from this particular project. It is okay to decide to switch to a project that interests you. The work on the original project is not wasted. The work you put into it helped you learn and grow. If the new version of you is excited by something else, go for it.

Tools to Give Yourself a Nudge

Make It New

When things are new, they are automatically more interesting than when they are familiar. Use this to your advantage with your existing projects. Making something about your project new can trigger increased interest and motivation. This could be as simple as changing your work location, using a different notebook, or trying a different tracking mechanism.

Make It Challenging

A variation on making things new is to make them challenging. This can take the form of setting a timer and seeing how much you can accomplish before it beeps. Or you can gamify your work. One of my kids gamified his math sheets by getting little figures and pretending they were having a race to complete the columns.

Making things challenging might frustrate the results-driven person, however, because it creates effort tangential to the task at hand.

Connect to an Interest

You probably have special interests, things that always draw your attention. Try seeing if you can connect the project you want work on to a special interest. Can you put birds into your novel? Can you add a crochet element to your visual art? Whatever draws you in can be used to get you moving on the work at hand.

Add Urgency

"Urgent" is why so many assignments and projects get scrambled together at the last minute. If urgency is high enough, suddenly the motivation and momentum show up. The timer mentioned in "Make it Challenging" created challenge through urgency. Deadlines automatically create urgency. A project that has been languishing for months or years will suddenly rush to completion when there is a deadline. This can be useful. You can set deadlines for yourself. If you struggle to keep yourself accountable, sign up for a conference or critique opportunity and use that as an external deadline. Even if you blow the deadline, you made progress, and the conference will still give you a chance to be in the company of other creative people, which can be a motivation all by itself. However, pay attention to the subtle difference between nudging yourself via urgency and driving yourself forward via anxiety.

Use Anxiety

There is no doubt that fear can be a huge motivator. The problem with using fear to get yourself moving is it puts you into fight or flight mode, which narrows your focus and can impede your ability to explore creatively. I covered anxiety as motivation in the last chapter. It has health consequences and creative costs.

Create Accountability

You can use the human tendency to want to fit in by setting up accountability for your creative projects. This could be as simple as body doubling, where you meet up with another person (either in person or online) to work in parallel. Being with another person who is working helps you stay on track with your own work. You can also set up more direct accountability by checking in on each other's progress.

Accountability to others might chafe at first for an internally motivated person (I know it often does for me), but can be really effective in getting you moving. A form of accountability I love is having a monthly check-in with other creative people where we talk about our work and what we hope to accomplish in the next month. Saying our plans out loud helps us follow through with those plans.

Get Angry

Anger gets a bad rap and is frequently labeled as a "negative" emotion. But anger isn't inherently bad; it becomes bad when people choose hurtful or impulsive actions because of the anger. Rachel Naomi Remen, a therapist and writer who works with terminal cancer patients, says that she is always glad to see anger in her patients. It means they're ready to fight rather than give up. Remen says: "Anger is just a demand for change, a passionate wish for things to be different."

Anger can be good fuel for good purposes. I know more than one author who has a "spite novel." It is the book they wrote to prove someone wrong, or it is a book they wrote to make a point to the world. I know writers who are angry about their life circumstances and write to escape them or to make sure no one else has to be alone with similar experiences. Sometimes, when people are stopped or hopeless, they need anger to get moving.

Find Your Why

Sometimes, the nudge you need to get you moving is to reconnect with the core purpose of your project. This is particularly important if you are emotionally motivated. To get moving, you need to feel connected to why your project matters to you or the world at large. This can take the form of remembering the needs of your intended audience, remembering the emotions you want your work to evoke, remembering that this work is a steppingstone to one of your dreams, or your own personal why. Finding the why for your specific project might lead you back to Chapter 2, *The Landscape of Dreams*, and Chapter 3, *Priorities*, but a smaller-scale activity included in this chapter will also help you explore it.

Activities

I'm offering a much larger array of activities than usual in a single chapter. Treat this like a choose-your-own adventure instead of homework list. Only do the activities that feel useful to you.

Motion Activity 1
Collecting the Pieces

Purpose : To give you extra impetus to reconnect with and get moving on a project after a long pause.

Collect the pieces of the project you want to restart into one place. If they're already in one place, pull them out and review them. If reviewing revives the ideas, feel free to brainstorm what comes next. If not, take a moment to write out why this project mattered. If you are still not feeling the project, carefully put everything away in a single place so you can find it again later. Or, bid it farewell and make space for something else in your life.

Motion Activity 2
Priming the Creative Engine

Purpose: To get you moving on a low-stakes creative effort so that once you're moving, you can switch to the work you want to get done.

Instead of trying to get moving on your big project, pick something low-stakes where you don't have to care about the result. Give yourself permission to play. Granting yourself this permission might be easier if you switch away from your regular medium. Pick something fun and permit yourself to be bad at it. A writer might try watercolor, a painter might knit, color in a coloring book or craft with clay. After ten or fifteen minutes of play, try your main project again and see if it comes easier to you.

Motion Activity 3
Finding Your Why

Purpose: To help you reconnect with the purpose of your creative project.

Grab writing tools or a friend to talk to and explore the following questions:

- What made you begin this project in the first place?
- What are the cool core ideas and themes?
- What do you hope this project will do in the world?
- What dream does completing this project help you move toward?

The next time you're struggling to get moving on your project, review this "why" page. Alternatively, create a visual representation of your "why" and put it someplace where you will see it.

MOTION ACTIVITY 4
THE BRAIN DUMP

Purpose: To clear your mind of distracting thoughts so you can focus on your creative projects.

Sit down and write about whatever comes to mind. Write about how you need to do dishes later today, how you're worried you'll miss your dentist appointment, or how the payment for that dental work is making you anxious about finances. Write thoughts as they come to you. You don't even have to write coherent sentences or connected thoughts. If it appears in your brain, write it down. You are dumping the contents of your brain out in your writing. When you're done writing, do you feel calmer? Do you have some action items? Often, I'm much more able to work on my creative projects after I've written a brain dump because all of my loose thoughts are now pinned down in words. An alternate version is finding a patient listener and talking through your brain dump instead of writing.

MOTION ACTIVITY 5
SPARK COLLECTION

Purpose: To help you connect with your creative project throughout the day so you're primed to work on it later.

As you move through your day, be on the lookout for a small detail you can add to your creative project: a snail on your path which becomes a spiral in stone in your work, or the turn of a person's head as they listen to a child that gets written into your current scene. These moments or objects can be sparks to add to your project. When you find a spark, note it down. This teaches your mind to always be looking for sparks to go in your work, and that remembering those sparks is important. It also connects your daily life to your creative project, making it easier to slide into working.

Motion Activity 6
The Project Playlist

Purpose: To use music to help you get moving on your creative project and then help you transition away from it at the correct time.

Make a playlist for your project that matches the length of time you have for a work session. Play your list whenever you work on your project to build an association between the music and the project. A well-timed playlist can gently remind you to leave hyperfocus mode and re-engage with the rest of your life.

Motion Activity 7
Challenging Wait Mode

Purpose: To give you practice at accomplishing tasks when you've dropped into wait mode.

Look at the scheduled event or task that has dropped you into wait mode. Calculate how much time you have between now and the onset of the task. Pick a chore or activity that will take less than half the time between now and then. Starting small can help. For example, if you have two hours, a fifteen-minute task is less likely to trigger anxiety than an hour-long task. If you accomplish four fifteen-minute tasks, you have successfully used your time in wait mode. With practice, you might be able to work up to tasks that take up a larger percentage of the available wait time.

If it feels useful, you might also spend some time writing about your wait mode experience. Ask yourself why you drop into wait mode, what purpose it serves, and how it feels to challenge it.

Motion Activity 8
Transition Practice

Purpose: To deliberately practice transitioning between tasks to see whether practicing transitions helps you improve.

Set aside half an hour and give yourself a list of three tasks. It might be useful to make one of the tasks be "Write about how this task switching is making me feel." Set a timer for five minutes and get started on a task; when the timer beeps, switch tasks immediately, even if you're halfway through folding a shirt. Do the second task for five minutes, switching to the third at the beep. Then repeat the cycle of tasks until your thirty minutes are done. Pay attention to your emotions around task switching. Do you have anxiety about the half-folded shirt? Does your brain try to do the equivalent of leaving a finger in the pages of a book so you can pick up where you left off? Observe how it feels when you return to the task after having done two other tasks. How frazzled do you feel when the half-hour is complete? Try this activity again on a different day and treat it as a deliberate exercise, like doing repetitions at the gym. Does task switching get easier with practice? Does the whole idea make you anxious? (If so, you might need other solutions instead of this one.)

Motion Activity 9
Experimentation

Purpose: To set up a deliberate experiment with one or more motivation tools.

Pick one of the tools listed above in "tools to get yourself moving" and make a plan for implementing it in your creative time. Some examples:

- You might plan rewards for yourself after you've done a set amount of work. (Feel free to buy those stickers or treats!)
- Set up deliberate accountability via body doubling or checking in and reporting.
- Gamify your work either by using apps designed for this (Habitica and Finch are ones I've tried) or by adding elements of challenge.

When you've done your experiment, reflect on whether the experiment helped you manage your motion. Use the reflection to consider what your next experiment might be.

Making Changes

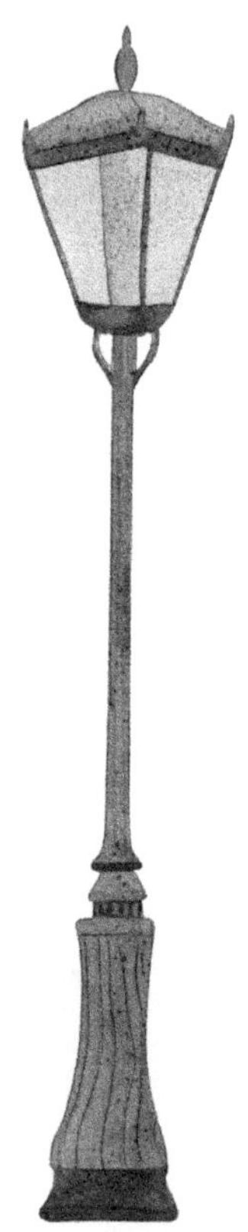

Chapter 16

Changing Your Life

I once visited a school that focused on helping autistic young adults learn skills for independent adulthood by giving them apartments and jobs on campus while offering classes. The staff of the school had a wide-ranging list of skills to teach, everything from personal sanitation to home maintenance to money management. All the teaching was done with clear expectations and no shame or judgment. If, during one of the weekly cleaning checks, a resident was found to have a very messy living space, the staff would gently confront them by saying something like, "Your system for laundry doesn't seem to be working. Shall we help you figure it out?"

So right here, at the beginning of this chapter on changing your life, I would like to invite you to adopt this tone with yourself. Some of your attempted changes are going to fall apart. Some of the habits you want aren't going to stick. Some of your intended transformation will yield to force of habit. When that happens, do not blame yourself. Simply recognize that the system you tried for making change did not work for you. Change always has a creative cost, but the long-term benefits for your life and creative projects can be great.

YOUR CREATIVE WORK THRIVES WHEN YOU CHOOSE YOUR CHANGES CAREFULLY AND BUILD STRUCTURE TO SUPPORT THOSE CHANGES.

The Change Cycle

Your path to make changes follows this pattern: Decision → Structure → Experiment → Evaluation → Iterate (New Decision).

Decision

Change starts with a decision. Your challenge is to direct that decision away from a vague "this has got to change" and towards focused knowledge of what to change and how soon. Be specific when deciding what to change.

Structure

Setting structure around the change you want can look like any of the following:

- **Setting goals.** One of the most common (and useful) tools for making changes is goal setting. This tool is so important that the next chapter will do a focused dive into how to set and implement good goals.
- **Recruiting accomplices.** Connect with your support network and find people to support you in your changes. If possible, you want people who will actively assist as well as cheer you on.
- **Setting up rails and boundaries.** We've talked in previous chapters about smoothing the path between you and the work you want to be doing. You can also install rails to guide you into it and away from falling into old habits. We'll give some examples of this later in the chapter.
- **Changing your calendar or commitments.** Look at your calendar and commitments to see what you need to shift to make room for create the change you want. Changing your calendar can help you avoid falling into an old habit.

These are only a few examples of structures you can put around the change you want. Feel free to think up your own ways to keep yourself focused on the change you want.

Experiment

Frame your attempts to change as an experiment. This will help you not take any failures personally. Set up your experiments in ways that let you measure results. Going for a walk after lunch each day to see if it improves your sense of well-being is good; pairing it with something that helps you track your sense of well-being is better. The tracking could be as simple as writing a sentence about how you felt at the end of each day. Your experiment should also have a set amount of time after which you will evaluate how it went.

Evaluation

I'm a big fan of evaluation. You can see this in many of my suggested activities where I give you a set amount of time and then an evaluation to determine if the activity works. Evaluation lets you adjust your efforts so they are better aimed. If your attempted change fell apart, evaluating can help you determine why. It lets you salvage any pieces of your change that you think were working so you can use them to craft your next experiment.

Evaluation can look like writing out your thoughts. It can look like a data-tracking graph. It can look like checking in with a support person to hear their thoughts on the change.

Evaluation returns you back to the beginning of the change process where you make a new decision: whether to continue your effort, discard your effort, or transform your effort into a new experiment.

Iterate (New Decision)

When you iterate, look at what happened before and decide what to adjust for in your next experiment. You should expect some of your changes to fail. This is fine. Failure is data from which you can form the next experiment.

When Life Shifts

Sometimes your systems fall apart, not because you're trying to change, but because something else in your life changes. Sometimes life hands you big changes. Life events like getting married, getting divorced, moving, changing jobs, and having a baby come to mind. Those sorts of events force you out of your old familiar patterns. Even a seemingly small shift can be significant. I had an example of small life shift just recently. I'd fallen into a lovely pattern of waking up, rolling out of bed, doing calisthenics, feeding cats, taking my meds, reading my scriptures, doing some writing, and then launching into the rest of my day. It all flowed smoothly, one task into another, feeling effortless. Then life changed. My husband started waking up at a different time, and I took a freelancing job that required morning meetings. My lovely morning pattern vanished overnight and left me wondering how to get it back. I tried to put it back via an exercise of willpower, but that effort also failed. I had to find other ways to feel centered and calm that fit my new life cadence.

Life patterns are always in flux. When your system falls apart, grab its best pieces and build a new system. (I put my writing time in during the evenings until the freelancing gig ended.) Having your schedule fall apart can be a gift, because sometimes it forces you to look at all the pieces and build something that works even better. When you know that falling apart is inevitable, you recognize that system failure is not a personal failure.

Transformational Change, Incremental Change

As you're considering the changes you want, you need to consider how much to change all at once. Movies and books sell total transformation as wonderful. We've all seen Cinderella. When your life is not what you want, you might be tempted to toss the whole mess and start over. The advantage of transformational change is that it is the shortest path between the life you have now and a new life that is much different. Sadly, transformation is hard on you, and it is hard on your support network. To support big changes, you have to adjust lots of structures all at once.

Something to consider when you're contemplating transformational change is whether you've set up your change for long term success. If you want to ditch your old life and live on a lake forever, you need long-term planning on how to pay your bills. If you're going to ditch your old life to live on a lake for a week, that requires a different set of plans.

In contrast, incremental change is easier on both you and your network. Setting aside two hours per week for your creative projects is much easier than quitting your job to go live in a house by a lake. Only you can decide what should be incremental or transformational in your life. For some people, setting aside two hours per week is a minor change; for others it requires lots of negotiation and shifting of commitments and priorities.

Small changes can feel frustrating because the results take time to be visible. Incremental change allows you to change a portion of your life and to let that change settle in before changing something else. Even very small changes can have significant ripple effects. Setting up a physical space for your creative efforts may be a small change, but having space allows you to make further changes. Now that you have space, you can signal you're busy or set creative triggers. An accumulation of small changes will, over time, result in a life transformation. Incremental changes are transformation in pieces and at a small scale over a longer time. In the fable The Tortoise and the Hare, it was the tortoise's incremental progress that eventually won the race. Both incremental and transformational change make life different.

You Have to Let Go

No matter how small or drastic the change you want to make, it requires you to let go of your old way of doing things. Sometimes, that comes easy, other times, it is quite difficult. When I had to update my online store software, I discovered that I also had to switch versions of my accounting software. I didn't want to; my accounting system was causing me no trouble, and learning a new way of accounting was work. But to fix my broken store system, I had to let go of a working accounting system. To get the changes you want, you may have to let go of things you like.

The Impact of Change on Others

Any change you make in your life will affect people around you. You need buy-in from the other people in your life in order to build the structure you need. Even with buy-in, the more changes you make at once, the more you will make other people in your life uncomfortable. As their discomfort increases, they may (consciously or unconsciously) pressure you to "return to normal." For this reason, massive life transformations can seriously disrupt relationships. Communication is critical during transformations, even if those transformations are made in small steps over time.

If you ask your network to support your changes, you should listen to them and support them in any changes they want. Much of this book encourages you to focus on what you need to build structure for your creative projects, but if you live in partnership with others, everyone's needs should be balanced against each other. Sometimes a change you want may need to wait for better timing. My lovely morning pattern could not exist when I had young children in school and my mornings had to be very regimented. Similarly, my desire for an office space that isn't shared must wait until a room in my house is vacated.

An Example of Implementing Change

Suppose you feel like you are spending too much time on social media sites. If you simply declare you're going to spend no more than an hour per day on social media but don't put any structure around that declaration, you're likely to fail. Instead, you could decide that any time you get on social media, you will set a one-hour timer. You now have a trigger to remind you to exit. However, you must use willpower and executive function to set the timer, and then you have to use willpower to turn off social media when the timer beeps. It is very easy to forget the timer or be distracted past the alarm. You can ask support people to help monitor your social media use, but this can cause friction between you and them. If, instead, you install nanny software that automatically limits your social media time to one hour per day, that has a much better chance at working because you are only making the decision once instead of daily. With the nanny software, if you want to extend your social media time, it requires another decision and an effort to do so. The nanny software is an example of installing a rail or boundary.

Up to this point, your efforts to change your social media habits are incremental changes because they mostly affect you. But if you want to put even more distance between you and social media, you can uninstall apps or deactivate accounts, thus making a significant logistical barrier to returning. An even more thorough method would be to completely cancel your Internet service. This last option would forcibly change many patterns in your life, have a significant impact on other members of your household, and create new problems. It would be a transformational effort.

Activities

Change Activity 1
A Small Change Cycle

Purpose: To practice the steps in the change cycle on something small so you can experience each step.

Pick one small change you want to implement. Follow the steps of the Change Cycle:

- **Decision.** Choose what you want to change.
- **Structure.** Design some structure around your change.

- **Experiment.** Perform your experiment by implementing the change.
- **Evaluation.** Evaluate how the change went.
- **Iterate (New Decision).** Adjust your plan and create your next experiment.

In your evaluation, take some time not only to evaluate the change itself but also the process of the change cycle. Are some steps easier for you than others? Do you need help with one of the steps? Can the change cycle be adapted to better fit how your brain and life work?

Change Activity 2
Considering Transformation and Conflict

Purpose: To help you think through the impact of your planned change.

If you are considering a change that might impact others, sit down with writing tools and write out the answers to each of the following questions.

- What inconveniences will your intended transformation cause for other people? What can you offer to decrease or balance those inconveniences with something positive for the other person?
- Are there regular conflicts you avoid instead of facing? What conversation and change would you like to have instead? (Note: look for places where you fall into patterns because they minimize and avoid conflict, not because the patterns are good for anyone.)
- Is there a conflict that needs to be resolved in your life? (Note: engaging with the conflict won't weaken relationships. Conflict exposes the weaknesses already there. Resolving conflicts through communication makes the relationships stronger.)

Chapter 17

Goals

When I was 29, I picked up writing again after a long fallow period. I was not ready to set goals; my dreams were still coalescing. As I wrote blog posts, stories, and essays, I discovered who I was as a writer. Over time, I started to know which direction I wanted to go with my projects and with my writing as a career. That was when I began to set goals. I visualized these goals as cobbles: each one small, but over time, if placed well, creating a path for me. This original conception is reflected in the name of my blog: *One Cobble at a Time* (https://onecobble.com/).

In the years since then, I have set many goals. Some I achieved, and some I abandoned or forgot. Over the years I've tried lots of different goals:

- When trying to teach myself discipline, I had a goal of writing at least 500 words per day and tracking this via a spreadsheet.
- When reeling from personal and financial blows and was trying not to lose track of my creative projects, my goal was to "touch any of my projects once per day" with a check box to say I'd done it.
- When mired in omnipresent anxiety, I set a goal to "be less afraid" and did not track it. I just set up visual cues so that when I started down an anxiety spiral, I could get off that ride and consciously choose to do something else with my attention.

Each of these goals matched my needs and priorities at the time. Some of them fell neatly into the form of a "good goal." (A form I'm about to describe to you.) Other goals broke those rules and landed in a space I'll describe later in this chapter as the "un-goal." The path I created out of goal cobbles meanders and sometimes seems haphazard. There are branches that lead nowhere because I backtracked. The turns in my path reflect my shifts as I changed dreams and adjusted for current priorities. Looking back at my path from a perspective of 20 years in building it, however, I can see how I now have fewer meanders and side paths because I learned how to form strong goals and keep them in alignment with my large-scale priorities and dreams. With practice I got better at building a path for myself to move forward. The building stones of that path are the goals I set.

YOUR CREATIVE WORK THRIVES WHEN YOU SET GOALS THAT ALIGN WITH YOUR PRIORITIES AND MOVE YOU TOWARD YOUR DREAMS.

What Makes a Good Goal

A good goal should set you up for success rather than failure. It should support you, not trap you inside its demands. Good goals have these core elements:

- **Alignment.** Your goals should be matched to your current priorities and carry you in the direction of your dreams.
- **Motivation.** A well-crafted goal should help you be excited to accomplish it. This means that when setting your goals, you'll need to dig into Chapter 14, *The Motivation Problem*, to make sure your goal supports your natural motivational modes. If external accountability chafes, then you should not set up goals requiring it or you'll be setting up the goal to fail.
- **Attainability.** A good goal is structured around what you control. A writer's goal to "get an agent" is not good because it requires another human to sign on to the deal. You can't

make someone else show up for you. Instead, "get an agent" should be defined as the dream (because dreams are allowed to be pie-in-the-sky unattainable). Your goal would be to submit queries to agents. You control whether or not you submit queries. You can't control the outcome of those queries.

- **Boundaries.** A well-bounded goal stays inside its lane and doesn't disrupt other priorities in your life. A goal that demands you keep a very strict schedule will create problems if the rest of your life tends not to be scheduled. If the goal is in support of a third-tier priority, you should be prepared to skip it in favor of tasks that serve your first-tier priorities. If the goal can't tolerate being skipped, it probably needs to be re-structured. For example, a goal of "write every day at 2 pm" probably won't work well for the parent of a toddler whose nap times are irregular. Instead, you may need to make your goal, "write when the baby sleeps."
- **Measurability.** Ideally, it is easy to tell when you have accomplished today's (or this week's or this month's) portion of the goal. In some of the goals I mentioned above, I had a tracking system to help me mark my progress. A goal to "be more mindful" is a mushy sort of goal, but a goal to meditate for ten minutes per day allows you to easily tell if you did today's goal task. This is not to say "be more mindful" is a bad life choice; it just falls under the role of an "un-goal" rather than a goal.
- **Checkpoints.** The best goals have built-in checkpoints where you evaluate whether the goal is properly serving you and your dream. Goals that are not serving properly should be altered or abandoned. Set checkpoints at the time you are setting up your goal.

Goal Check-Up

You probably arrived at this book with some goals already in your life. You may have already changed or altered some of them in response to ideas you have learned while reading this book. Now is a great time to scan your calendar, to-do lists, and memory for all of your existing goals to consider whether they're actually serving your highest priorities and dreams. Do your pre-existing goals meet the standards of a good goal? Perhaps it is time to excuse some of them from your life.

Abandoning a Goal

Goals are always a means to an end, not the end itself. If maintenance on a goal is absorbing too much energy or keeping you from working on your projects, that goal needs to be reconsidered. Above, I described several goals I set for myself and then abandoned when my needs changed. Abandoning a goal does not mean I failed at the goal. My "write 500 words a day" goal was very useful to me until my anxiety spiked; then, I needed to switch my focus to being less afraid. Learning to be less afraid helped me untangle many unprocessed emotions, which helped creativity flow more smoothly. When you let go of a goal, it can feel like failure. In that moment, you need to tell yourself a story about the change. For my goal shift, instead of "I'm so bad at this I couldn't even keep up 500 words a day," I said, "Look how far 500 words a day got me, but I need to shift my focus now."

You should have a periodic check-in on your goals see how they connect to your priorities and dreams. If your "fold laundry every week" goal connects to your "keep my space tidy" priority, it is a perfectly aligned goal. However, if "fold laundry every week" is only floating there on your list because someone taught you it is a task that should be done, maybe it doesn't get to be on your list anymore. The world is full of functional adults who let their clean laundry live in hampers.

Another example of a goal not serving the goal setter is my friend who decided to learn a new language via an online app. At first, she loved the setup and the fact the app had built-in goals like "maintain your learning streak." Over time, she discovered she was more focused on maintaining the streak than on learning the language. The app's built-in goal structure was causing stress and pulling her away from her dream of learning the language.

She changed her goal to playing the language games six days per week. Then, she would take a day off to rest and deliberately break the tyranny of the streak. She also added a once-per-month check to see if app-based learning was sufficient or if she needed some real-world instruction.

Sometimes other people assign goals to you, ostensibly to help you reach your dreams, but those goals can cause friction because they're mismatched to your needs and natural modes of progression. Don't be shy about rejecting or altering goals imposed on you by others.

The Un-Goal

An un-goal is like a goal in that it serves to help you move forward, but is missing some of the aspects of a good goal. When I decided I needed to "be less afraid," I was reluctant to call my effort a goal because it did not have the required attainability or measurability. Calling my efforts a goal created exactly the sort of anxiety I was trying to escape. Then, I attended a yoga class. The teacher was encouraging and accepting. The class was a community one with a mix of long-time enthusiasts and newbies. With every motion the teacher described, she would add instructions like, "Reach for your toes; it is okay if you can't touch them. That doesn't matter, just reach in the direction of them. The reaching is what matters." So, I reached for my toes, and I breathed. I felt the stretch and the calm. The practice was what I needed, not the achievement.

If you have trauma about goals, I suggest you ignore any or all of the "rules" for goal setting and instead set "un-goals" or practices in your life. Find ways of *being* and *enjoying* rather than focusing on accomplishing. This is what I did while trying to "be less afraid." I put practices in my life to help me with that. My needs and capacities shifted as I gained skill and strength with those practices. When I'd rested and healed, I was ready to set achievement-focused goals again. For me, returning to goal setting was a return to wholeness. Others may want and need a different way to be whole. Goals have very specific power to help you move along a path toward your dreams, but motion is not the be-all-end-all of existence. Sometimes, particularly when a person is grieving or healing, stillness is of greater value than motion. You move better when rested and healthy. You can rest until moving sounds joyful again. There is nothing wrong with living a life that is not focused on achievement.

Failing at Goals

Remember: a goal is a way of making change in your life. I discussed last chapter that many of your attempted changes will fail. So will many of your attempted goals. When a goal falls apart, use the change cycle to reformulate it into a new goal or abandon it because it no longer serves you.

Activities

Goals Activity 1
Goals List

Purpose: To look at your goals and see how they match your priorities and dreams.

Set up a page with two columns. In the left-hand column, write down your current goals. As you make this list, scan your calendar, task list, or memory for any efforts that are goal-like, even if you never thought of them as goals. Are you trying to keep your kitchen spotless? Write it down as a goal. Hoping to finish a project by a certain deadline? That's a goal, too. Some of these may end up being more un-goal-like when we're done. Don't try to evaluate that at this point. For now, only include the goals you're currently implementing, not new ones you think you might want to add.

Write these goals down without judgment, even if you're failing at living up to them. You may end up with a very short *Goals List* or an unrealistically long one. Either result is fine.

In the right-hand column, write down the priority or dream each goal moves you toward. You can use your previously created priorities and dreams lists to help. If you find goals that are unconnected to a priority or dream, pause and examine why they exist in your life. Do they reveal a priority or dream that was previously hidden? Or, are they there because someone else told you they should be?

GOALS ACTIVITY 2
DEEP DIVE

Purpose: To do a deep dive into a single goal to determine if it serves you well. Then, if this process is helpful, to repeat it with other goals.

Pick one goal that feels important or has a significant footprint in your life and ask the following questions. (If it helps, you can do a free write on these questions.)

- What dream does the goal move you toward?
- Does it contribute toward a sense of progression in your life?
- Where does the goal create friction?
- Can you modify the goal to reduce or remove the friction?
- What would be the consequences of abandoning this goal?
- Could it be replaced with a goal that better moves you toward the dream?

Write as much or as little as you want for each question. When you're done, consider whether this goal analysis helped you gain valuable insights. If it didn't, move onward. If it did, consider doing similar deep dives on other goals in your life.

Goals Activity 3
Setting New Goals

Purpose: To implement a new goal in your life. (Skip this activity if the thought of adding more goals feels stressful.)

Look through the sections of this book for inspiration and think of 1-3 goals you would like to implement.

Next, pull out your existing goals list. Is there something you can knock off your list to make energy and space for the new goal?

Use the structure described in Chapter 16, *Changing Your Life,* to build some structure around the new goal you want to have. Make sure to do the evaluation step after your experiment.

Special Cases to Consider

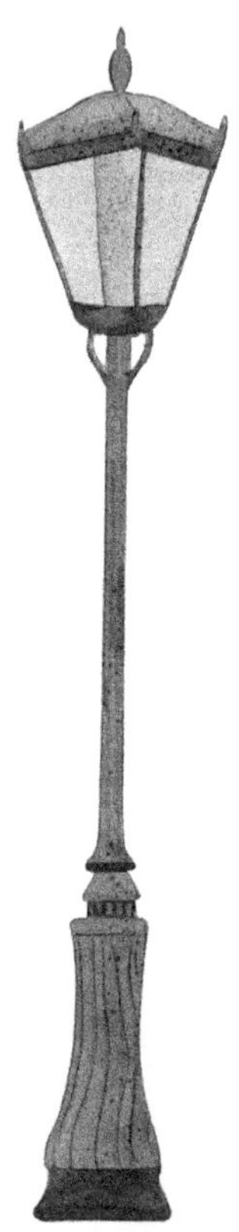

Chapter 18

Cultivating Confidence

I once was able to attend a writing conference on a cruise ship. The formal nights on the ship gave me an excuse to dress up for dinner. One evening, after eating, I decided to walk on the deck in the open air. I thought perhaps I could stroll all the way forward to look over the bow of the ship and see the ocean ahead. It is possible I thought I could spread my arms wide and feel like I was flying, like the characters in the *Titanic* movie.

I quickly discovered how incredibly windy it can be on deck when the ship is traveling at speed. Instead of a leisurely, glamourous stroll, I found myself clutching parts of my clothing to keep them attached. I quickly found shelter behind one of the many wind baffles that exist on deck. The baffle blocked enough of the wind to let me catch my breath and finally look up to see the stars. Instead of strolling, I sat, enjoying the open air in a protected spot. Then, I planned my path to get myself back inside before I was completely in shambles.

I thought about that windy cruise experience on a very different day when I was safe at home. It was a day of high anxiety, my thoughts swirling and pushing at me from every side. Self-doubt, imposter syndrome, and fears for the future all tugged and pressed so I could barely do anything except hold tight and try not to lose my grip on the items I didn't want to lose. When the storm subsided and I was able to breathe again, I realized what I needed was a set of baffles designed to shelter me from the winds of self-doubt — something I could use to protect me from those winds and make me able to enjoy the space instead of fleeing from a buffeting.

Over the years, I've managed to create shelter for myself, and I've learned how to make there be less self-doubt by developing self-confidence. Your creative work thrives when you build structures to protect your projects from self-doubt, and you cultivate a belief in the value of your projects.

> YOUR CREATIVE WORK THRIVES WHEN YOU LEARN TO CHALLENGE YOUR SELF-DOUBT AND CULTIVATE CONFIDENCE.

Voice of Self-Doubt

In order to buffer against wind, you first need to know where the wind is coming from. Pause a moment and reflect on this question: **In whose voice does your self-doubt speak to you?**

If your self-doubt has the voice of a specific person (perhaps a parent, teacher, or sibling), you may still be carrying a hurt inflicted by that person from earlier in your life. Healing that hurt and quieting your self-doubt may require you to apply some boundaries as is covered in the Chapter 6, *The Boundaries You Need*. Just because someone said something critical about your work doesn't make that criticism true. If the voice of your self-doubt is specifically that of a single person, then your task is to make that person's opinion of your work irrelevant. Their opinion can go sit in the corner while you're working on your projects. Ask yourself if that person is infallible and correct at all times. Then ask yourself why you are letting one person's criticism stop your projects.

If your self-doubt is a homebrewed voice that is either a combination of many people's criticism or your own self-criticism, the task is similar. You need to make a space between the self-doubt and your projects. You need to hold the self-doubt at bay and give your projects room to grow.

When and how does your self-doubt show up? Observing which situations make self-doubt noisy may lead you to its sources. By performing this observation and introspection on my own self-doubt, I discovered I was tying my self-worth to actions rather than believing I had value independent of them. Your self-doubt may have different root causes than mine. There might be big traumatic experiences feeding it. There might be a collection of small experiences over time.

Grant Yourself Messiness

When my children were small, I filled my house with paper and crayons. The crayons outlasted the boxes they came in, so I ended up with a plastic bin full of loose (often broken) crayons. I bought construction paper and tape in bulk packs. There were craft boxes full of interesting bits and bobs. These supplies existed in my house not because the resulting crafts were artistically important, but because making crafts was a source of joy to my children. They learned from each craft they made. Fine motor skills, cutting skills, learning to visualize in 3D — all of these crafts helped my children grow. I cheerfully tossed crayons, paper, tape, and scissors onto the altar of that growth. Growth was the point.

Grant yourself the same grace to explore as I gave to my children. Let go of the idea that the determining factor between "waste" and "well-spent" is the result rather than the process. This may be hard for you when you know the creative materials must come from the same accounts as food for your table. If your resources feel scarce, you may be wary of how you spend them. If you can recognize that you are spending on growth instead of a finished project, the knowledge can help you allow yourself some "wasted" materials. (Hint: they aren't wasted any more than water is wasted when used to nurture a plant.)

When you allow self-doubt to stop your creative explorations, you slow down your creative growth. If you look at your work and think, "This isn't good enough," stop and ask yourself, "Isn't good enough for what?" A creative project doesn't have to be "good enough" to be worth doing. You may be correct that your current project isn't good enough to achieve your dream. But if your response to your project not being good enough is to stop trying, you have cut off your growth. Your work isn't good enough…yet. So, give yourself resources and time to practice.

Granting yourself space to create without judgment is like setting up a baffle to protect you from the headwinds of self-doubt. You can spend time and resources on projects just because you enjoy them without requiring them to have any further use.

Qualifications and Skills

For some people, self-doubt centers around skill. This is often framed as Impostor Syndrome, which is the belief you are not qualified but have somehow fooled people into letting you do the work anyway. Imposter Syndrome can also manifest as a pervasive sense of not belonging. When you doubt your qualifications, asking yourself the following questions might help:

- **Will your lack of skill do damage?** For most pursuits, the answer is no. When there is a risk of damage there is usually some sort of certification process. A poorly crafted novel or painting does not injure other people. Your lack of expertise harms no one. Continue with your work.
- **Can you acquire skills as you go?** Identify the skills you need and deliberately set out to learn them. No one becomes an expert without a learning process. You can gain skills by doing. You can seek out resources and tutorials to help.

Remember: someone out in the world is making projects with fewer skills and qualifications than you. They're out there doing it *confidently* and *badly*. You can do something better than what is already available. Use that knowledge as a shield against your self-doubt.

Who Does Your Project Serve?

One of the ways I learned to dance around my self-doubt was to not focus my attention on my skills or qualifications but instead to laser focus on my intended audience. Who was I creating my book for, and how did I hope to help them? When I'm focused on who I'm helping, I focus less on myself. It helps me move past feeling unqualified because I'm answering a need. Imagining this book being useful gave me courage enough to write it.

If, when you consider who your work serves, the answer is only you, that does not make the work less worthy. Your projects bring you joy and growth. There is a beautiful strength in claiming time, effort, and space to do something only for you. Knowing who your project serves (even if just you), can shelter you from self-doubt.

What if No One Cares?

What if you pour your soul into a project that you want to share, but then no one pays any attention? What if your triumphant launch falls flat? Fear of future rejection can cause you to doubt the value of your projects. Sometimes to the point of abandoning them. When you feel stopped because you fear future rejection or pain, remember this: the future reception of your project does not matter to the work you need to do today. No matter how the work is received, making your project helps you grow. Anything helping you grow is worth doing.

Sometimes, when you try to share your creations with people, they are underwhelmed or turn away. This does not necessarily reflect on the value of your project. Your project may have an audience problem — those people are not the right audience for your project. This can be the case even if the people are close to you in your life. My husband was two years into drawing his comic before I really saw him as an artist. That's how long it took for my mental picture of who he was to catch up to the work he'd done. Putting your project in front of different people might get very different results.

Cultivating Self-Confidence

I once heard my friend (a literary agent) say that authors need to have an unhinged self-confidence in order to push through all the resistance offered by life and the publishing industry. I felt some truth in my friend's words, but I was also incredibly uncomfortable. "Unhinged self-confidence" is not something I have naturally. I am very wary of intense self-confidence, especially since it often comes paired with a willingness to step on others to achieve personal goals. Yet my friend, who is very smart, was advocating for this sort of confidence, saying it was essential to succeed at writing a book. I took my discomfort with self confidence and did some research to help me find ways to have the necessary confidence to push a project forward without becoming the person who steamrolls others.

Self-confidence is clearly the antidote to self-doubt. The good news is that while self-confidence cannot be acquired like a pair of shoes or a new book, it is something you can gain through practice. The more you work on developing your self-confidence, the more confidence will be available when you need it. When you practice confidence as a skill, you can also be mindful of how you wield your confidence. You can use your acquired confidence to uplift and build. Once I realized that, I understood why my friend advocated for it and I practiced confidence to build as much skill as I could acquire. Here are some ways to practice self-confidence:

- **Separate yourself from your creative projects.** Recognize that your value is not dependent on what you do or the skill level you have. The success or failure of your creative project does not reflect your value. The success or failure of a particular project speaks only to that particular project and to the time, place, and people with whom it was shared. Recognizing and remembering this can protect you from critiques both harsh and mild.

- **Learn to accept praise.** When someone compliments you or your work, learn to say "thank you" instead of dodging the compliment. If saying "thank you" is uncomfortable, sit with the discomfort and think about where it comes from. Remember: praise is a gift. You need to honor that gift rather than minimizing or denying it. You can use "separating yourself from your creative projects" to make accepting praise more comfortable. Their praise is about them and the project, not you. When people tell me they like my book *Hold on to Your Horses*, my answer is, "Thank you! I'm always happy when Amy (the main character) makes new friends." I also speak highly of the illustrator for the project. "I got such a great artist!"
- **Learn to praise your own skill and work.** This behavior is often negatively labeled as "bragging." But there is a big difference between speaking confidently and bragging. Bragging inserts your accomplishments into a conversation where they don't belong and often seeks to make someone else look bad in comparison. This is rude and is why bragging gets a bad reputation. If it helps, remember to separate yourself from your work. You may be able to speak confidently about part of your project, an idea, or a character ("My story has these really cool magical trees.") while directly speaking of your skill can feel harder ("I'm really good at dialogue."). When you speak confidently about your projects, you set the tone for the people around you to value those projects. Learn to speak of your work with praise and joy.
- **Absorb confidence from others.** Among your support network, you (hopefully) have people who believe in your work and your skills. Try to let those voices replace the voice that speaks self-doubt to you. If you can't believe in yourself, you can lean on the belief others have in you. Stay close to the people who believe in you until you can see in yourself what they see.
- **Collect evidence of value.** When someone says something nice about your work, write it down. Remember the moment your friends' faces lit up when they saw you; that

instantaneous gladness isn't faked. If you have a moment when you feel your work is good, make a note of it. Perhaps use a special notebook to catch these moments. This will train your brain to notice and keep the good moments instead of storing up "evidence" that feeds your self-doubt.

- **Do it scared.** If you are a person who lives with self-doubt and fear, trying to quell all fears before proceeding is a recipe for getting stuck. Learn to create despite the fear. Courage is not the absence of fear. Courage is the decision to act in defiance of fear.
- **Be mindful of others.** In cultivating self-confidence, you do not want to become someone whose confidence takes all the space in the room and impedes the growth of others. As you gain strength, make sure you're using that strength to lift others. Use your confidence to speak confidently about other people's projects.
- **Own your mistakes.** Mistakes are inevitable; no one charts a flawless path through their creative projects or life. Like your projects, your mistakes are not reflective of your value. If you waste energy trying to hide your mistakes, you will live in fear of their discovery. If, instead, you own your mistakes, there is no dramatic reveal, no unmasking of the impostor. Being skilled and confident means learning from the inevitable mistakes, not being mistake-free. Mistakes are a necessary part of the learning journey, and you can learn from them better when you own up to them.

Activities

Confidence Activity 1
The Voice of Self Doubt

Purpose: To help you identify the specific voices your self-doubt uses so you can take further steps to counteract them.

For your next creative work session, bring a notebook or writing tool that is not used for your usual process. As you work, whenever you find yourself with a negative or self-doubting thought, write it down — just make a quick note of what the thought is and a bit about what you were doing when the thought showed up. Then look at the note, tell it you'll deal with it later, and get on with the creative work for the session.

When your creative session is over, take a closer look at your self-doubt notes. Is there a pattern in the types of thoughts that show up in particular aspects of your work? Take one of the thoughts and set a timer for five minutes. During those minutes, write about where you think the thought comes from. Did an incident in your life seed this self-doubt? Did a person criticize you in a particular way that you've now internalized to criticize yourself? What evidence or practice can you put into place as a shield against future instances of this self-doubt?

You may want to repeat the exercise with your self-doubt notebook to see if there are different patterns over time. Just remember that you're recording in order to address and dismiss. If, instead, the recording causes you to focus more on your negative thoughts, this practice may not be best for your brain.

Confidence Activity 2
Name the Person Who Needs Your Project

Purpose: To perform a thought experiment to help those who struggle to believe in their own value and the value of what they create.

Think of an artist, musician, or author whose work affected you deeply and whom you've never met or thanked. If you want, you can do a five-minute writing session exploring what that person's creation means to you and what you would say if you had the chance to thank them.

Now look at your own project and consider that there is a person out in the world who needs your unique project as much as you needed the work of the artist about whom you wrote.

Do another writing session imagining a person who needs your project and who will be helped by what you create. Whose problem do you want to solve? Who do you want to make laugh?

To what child do you want to give a story? To whom does your work reach? It is perfectly valid if the answer is yourself.

Confidence Activity 3
Collecting Evidence

Purpose: To deliberately gather evidence that your work is worth doing.

Create a space to deliberately collect your work's praise and bright moments. This can be a special notebook, folder on your computer, Pinterest board, or other tool that lets you quickly access the records. One visual artist made drawings that caught good moments and put them together in a collage. They could then view the collage from afar on hard days.

When you're having a day where self-doubt is loud, review the evidence. If, when looking through the collection, your brain discounts it or tells stories about how this doesn't count, stop yourself. The flow should be in the other direction. You collected these moments because they are real. They happened. They're evidence the self-doubt is wrong.

Confidence Activity 4
Practicing Praise

Purpose: To consciously practice speaking confidently about yourself and the value of your creative projects.

Pick a thing you do that makes you happy or you feel you're good at. Then, praise yourself for doing it. For example, if you enjoy dancing in your kitchen while cleaning, say out loud, "I'm good at dancing. It makes me happy." It does not matter if you are good at it on some (imaginary) good dancer scale; you're good at the kind of dancing that makes you happy in your kitchen.

Self praise can be uncomfortable. Sit with the discomfort, think about where it comes from, and see if you feel less uncomfortable with practice.

Chapter 19

Your Access Needs

When my mother was thirteen, she received her first pair of glasses. Her eyesight had been bad for a while but, due to some chaotic life circumstances, it took years before an adult noticed and got her the glasses. When she put them on, she was amazed to realize that trees had individual leaves and weren't just a big green blur. A simple adaptive tool made her world easier, richer, and more complex.

Not all of us need glasses, but we can all benefit from adaptive tools. In fact, tools like jar openers, step stools, canes, mobility devices, ramps, and elevators are so common that we don't think of them as adaptive tools at all. If you are one of the fortunate few without adaptive tools at this point in your life, all it takes is a sprained ankle to change that condition. Adaptive tools can't negate all disadvantages but deploying them can help make more space and time for your creative projects.

YOUR CREATIVE WORK THRIVES WHEN YOU SEEK OUT AND USE ADAPTIVE TOOLS TO OVERCOME YOUR CHALLENGES.

Recognizing Challenges

Before you can deploy adaptive tools to make your life easier (and make more space for your creative work), it helps if you recognize your challenges.

In prior chapters, you spent time identifying your challenges and making changes to adapt for them. You found the friction points and smoothed them as you went. Now is the time for you to step back and look at what your challenges have in common. For example, you might discover that your struggles with losing craft supplies, forgetting appointments, and making decisions are all related to a core challenge: working memory. Naming a core challenge means you can begin to address the source rather than playing whack-a-mole with its many manifestations.

Some common core challenges for creative people are:

- **Time blindness.** Some people have an innate sense of when time has passed. Other people don't. Even the people who generally sense time can lose track if they get deep into creative flow or they're overburdened with tracking too much.
- **Sensory sensitivities.** Some people are prone to overstimulation. When there are too many inputs, the brain seeks out rest from those inputs, either by seeking a space with less input or shutting down. Sometimes, you don't even realize you're becoming overstimulated until you get away from the stimulus. An example is when you encounter silence and solitude after a busy day and experience relief. Other people might suffer when there isn't enough stimulus and then seek to make their own by adding motion or noise.
- **Object permanence.** Some people tend to forget things that are out of sight (the buried bill, the food in the back of the fridge) while other people can hold hidden objects in memory. But even if you're normally good at tracking, a period of stress can cause you to lose track of things. In addition to the lost objects, spoiled food, and other impacts to daily living, this losing track of things can have an emotional impact.
- **Working memory.** Working memory is like a desktop in your brain, the space you use to organize, plan, manipulate, and transform information. Some people have a spacious desktop that can hold multiple projects simultaneously. Others have a small available workspace; if they pull one

thing to the center they may knock several other things off the desk completely.

- **Limited executive capacity.** While working memory is the ability to calculate and manipulate information, executive capacity is the ability to make decisions and execute a plan. Some people have a sizeable capacity to make decisions and push themselves to do unpleasant tasks. Other people become overwhelmed after only a few choices and tasks.
- **Particularity.** Some people strongly need to see things done in a specific way or see things done "right." For the particular person, when the world is wrong, they either shut down to avoid dealing with it or take action to correct things. Particularity often goes with perfectionism, but not always.
- **Perfectionism.** This is the driving need to make sure your work is perfect. Perfectionism usually has a deeply emotional component. Often the emotion is fear of ridicule or consequences that might occur if the work is imperfect. If you're driven by perfectionism, it can strongly impact your life and creative projects.
- **Tight finances.** We all have very real limits on the funds available to pursue our creative work. If your creative project has a budget of zero dollars, that is a challenge that must be planned around and coped with. A lack of funds doesn't indicate a lack of importance.
- **Tight time scheduling.** Similar to limited finances, some people have lives where their time is tightly scheduled and whose creative work will only get done when it is shoehorned in somewhere.
- **Chronic health condition or illness.** Our health or lack thereof impacts every aspect of our lives. The challenges of coping with chronic health issues and illness are explored more fully in Chapter 21, *Health Challenges and Creativity*.
- **Caregiving**. Taking care of others, whether it's providing occasional emotional support or ongoing physical care, can have a significant impact on the amount of creative energy you have available for your projects. The challenges of caregiving in a creative life are explored in more detail in Chapter 20, *Caregiving and Creativity.*

- **Something else.** As you read through my list, you may have thought, "But what about ______?" There are more possible challenges than I have space to list, and I am limited by my current knowledge in imagining all the possible challenges you might face. But the concepts of creating access and adapting for challenges are useful, no matter what shape your challenges take.

The Case for Diagnosis

I deliberately listed these challenges in general terms without attaching any sort of diagnosis to them. This is because I am neither licensed nor qualified to hand out diagnoses. I do want to put in a positive word for seeking out a diagnosis for yourself if you are facing consistent daily struggles meeting expectations. Diagnosis can be valuable even if you never intend to make that diagnosis public. When you face consistent challenges, diagnosis is a key that opens up new toolboxes to help you cope with the challenges you have. In addition, there is power in knowing and naming your particular challenges. Diagnosis also can provide tools for your support network so they can understand and support you better. My mother was muddling through and making do with the sight available to her. Diagnosis and prescription glasses opened up a whole new world and gave her a life-long tool that changed her trajectory.

If you don't need diagnosis, or if you're not ready to seek one, you can gain a lot of benefit from looking into the tools deployed by people who have diagnoses. I'm very fond of sending creative people to look at the tools used by people who have ADHD, OCD, autism, and anxiety. Many of those tools are universally useful.

Finding Tools

Whether or not you seek a diagnosis, you need tools to help you adapt to the core challenges of your life. My house includes adaptive tools for every challenge I listed above. Finding those adaptive tools was a process. That process will never be complete because new tools are created all the time and new challenges will pop up while others fade away. Learning the process for finding tools is far more valuable to you than a (necessarily incomplete) listing of tools. To demonstrate the process, I'll take you through a search for tools relating to "working memory."

- **Do an internet search.** In the search engine of your choice, enter the words "working memory" + the word "adaptations" and see what comes up. You can also try variations like "working memory" + "problem-solving" or "working memory" + "tricks and tips" Be aware that the internet is filled with bad information along with good, so before you apply any suggestions, vet the source. A medical research center is more likely to have useful information for you than a company wanting to sell a product. At the moment I'm writing this book, most internet searches lead off with "AI answers," which are dubious. Read further down the list to find more complex and nuanced responses. If the source you're looking at also cites other sources, that is a positive sign.
- **Refine your searches and repeat.** Suppose in your first search you find information describing working memory as a mental desk. You could now try searching "working memory adaptations desk." That leads to more articles expanding upon the idea of working memory as a desk. You discover that the size of the desktop you have available for a given day is variable. Some days you may have a spacious mental desk and others a small one. Also, for some people, "knocked off the desk" means they can find it and pick it up tomorrow, but for other people, "knocked off the desk" means the thing disappeared into a bottomless void, never to be found again. This additional information is great, but ultimately, the true treasure of your research will be to find a subject matter expert.
- **Identify your experts.** Your expert could be a book, a coaching professional, a therapist, a website, a focused YouTube channel, or an experienced friend. You're looking for someone with extensive knowledge and the ability to

help you see your challenges in new ways and to teach you coping techniques. Some experts will explain exactly how to apply those techniques. Others will be more focused on knowledge and theory, leaving specific adaptations for you. Sometimes, the value of an expert is that you bounce off their advice in a way that sends you in a new, useful, direction.

- **Perform experiments.** At this point in the book, performing an experiment based on new information should feel familiar. In this case, I won't give you an activity assignment, you can create your own "activity" based on the research you did and the problem you're trying to solve. For the example I use, working memory, perhaps you could use task clumping (as described in *Managing Mental Load*) to stack your tasks so they take up less space. You could also deploy some alarms and set up visual reminders to help you put things you've forgotten back onto your mental desk.
- **Involve your network.** At every stage of this process, you can involve your support network to help you figure out your challenges and how to address them. Some of your support network might be your experts. Even if they are not experts in your particular challenge, having someone to listen while you describe and troubleshoot your problems can make a huge difference in finding solutions.

Searches for answers frequently lead to unexpected places. Your search for adaptive tools to work with your challenges may lead you away from what is described in my example. This is perfectly fine. Follow your own search path.

What comes next is a set of starting points to launch you into finding more tools for various challenges. When you find the right tools, your "challenge" can be a strength or benefit in your life. Sometimes what needs to be changed is not the behavior but the structure that creates friction around an innate tendency and turns it into a problem instead of a strength.

Time Blindness

Research terms: Time blindness, temporal myopia, time perception difficulties.

Suggested adaptations: Alarms and bells are your friend, as is a clock that chimes audibly on every hour or half hour. Hang clocks where you can see them.

Sensory Sensitivities

Research terms: Hypersensitivity, sensory overload, hyperesthesia, sensory dysregulation.

Suggested adaptations: Develop strategies and practices to help you return to a centered and regulated state. Weighted blankets, trampolines, swinging chairs, headphones, and eye masks are all tools with a common thread: they put you in control of the sensory input instead of leaving you reacting to inputs you can't control. Practice over time can help you develop skills at re-regulating yourself with smaller and more portable interventions.

Object Permanence

Research terms: Object permanence.

Suggested adaptations: Arrange your physical spaces so you can see your tools or physical reminders of your tasks. Don't place things behind each other or stack them because the hidden objects may be forgotten. Create landing zones or homes for important objects, like keys, which you need to keep track of so you can build patterns around them. Have a "loading zone" by the front door where you place things you need to take when you leave.

Working Memory

Research terms: Working memory, short-term memory, operative memory.

Suggested adaptations: Many of the suggestions in Chapter 7, *Managing Mental Load*, include systematic reminders, and task clumping. Use physical or visual reminders to help you remember tasks.

Limited Executive Capacity

Research terms: Executive function, cognitive control, supervisory attentional system.

Suggested adaptations: Task clumping, pre-deciding and other possible adaptations are fully covered in the Chapter 7, *Managing Mental Load.* The key is to reduce decision-making and the need for willpower in your daily life.

Particularity

Research terms: Perfectionism, ordering compulsion, excessive organizing.

Suggested adaptations: Adaptations for particularity are dependent on the way it is expressed or interfering in your life. Sometimes the need to have things a certain way may be related to an unconscious need for accessibility. What may seem like pickiness about types of lights may be a sensory sensitivity to those lights.

Perfectionism

Research terms: Perfectionism, self-doubt.

Suggested adaptations: Adaptations for perfectionism depend on what emotion is making you afraid to do less than perfect work. Practicing at tasks where the result doesn't matter may help you learn how to not perfect everything.

Tight Finances

Research terms: Limited budget, frugality, low income, include "free" or "low cost" + your local town in your search strings.

Suggested adaptations: When you don't have the money, it limits your ability to pay for supplies, classes, and opportunities that would help forward your creative work. The good news is that the path you can't afford is not the only path forward; you can build a different one. Search for free local resources. Connecting with others to build community around shared or low-cost resources helps you and others.

Tight Time Scheduling

Research terms: Time management, overscheduled.

Suggested adaptations: I unpack a lot of adaptations for scheduling in Chapter 10, *Curating Your Commitments*, and Chapter 13, *Time Scheduling and Project Management*.

Chronic Health Conditions or Illness

Research terms: Use research terms related to the symptoms or diagnoses you're coping with. Be cautious — searching medical issues can cause you to focus on dire and unlikely outcomes.

Suggested adaptations: Please check Chapter 21, *Health Challenges and Creativity*, for a deeper discussion.

Caregiving

Research terms: Caregiver burnout, terms specific to your situation like "eldercare" or "childcare."

Suggested adaptations: Please check Chapter 20, *Caregiving and Creativity*, where I explore the impacts and adaptations in full.

Activities

Access Activity 1
Your Challenges List

Purpose: To explore and reflect on your challenges, especially if you have challenges that did not appear on the above lists.

Sit down with writing tools and list challenges you have that impact your life. This list will likely be more useful to you if you're specific instead of general. Write down "the sound of other people's pencils in class" instead of the more general "I have sensory sensitivities." Being specific about challenges gives you a better handle on finding adaptations for them later.

If making this list (or any items on the list) trigger emotions in you, take some time to write and reflect on those emotions so you can see and process them.

Access Activity 2
The Adaptation Process

Purpose: To apply the tool-finding process described in this chapter to one of your challenges.

Select one of the challenges on your list and go through the research process described above to find adaptive tools that you think might help. Create your own activity or experiment to apply your chosen tool for a set amount of time. Then, reflect on whether the tool helped you in the way you hoped.

Chapter 20

Caregiving and Creativity

Through all of my adult life, my creative work of writing has been impacted by the care work I do for others. Primary care of young children turned into emotional support care for neurodivergent teenagers, then into less intensive support care for young adults. During all those years, I participated in various church and writer communities where I provided service that absorbed time and energy. Then came my husband's Long COVID disability, which required re-apportioning the load of tasks we carry between us. My parents are in their eighties and highly independent, but in the next few years I may need to make space in my life for elder care. Then there is the care I must supply for myself to manage the strict diet my auto-immune disorder requires. All of this weighs heavily on me even before my anxiety imagines things that might happen but haven't happened yet.

Care work is hard. When I look at my task lists in my notebook, I can see the daily impact of my care for others. Care work is also hugely creative. It requires problem-solving, advance planning, adaptability in the face of unexpected change, and large amounts of emotional labor. As stated in Chapter 1, *On Creative Work*, any creative effort you have in your life draws from the same creative well as every other creative process in your life. This care work can drain your creative pools completely and leave you with nothing available. Even when the work is routine and daily, it still draws from your available energy and time.

Yet, this work is important. It is needed. The world needs people to step up and take care of others. If you are a caregiver, thank you so much for being one of the people who is willing to show up and give care. The work you're doing may be actual life or death for the person, creature, or task being cared for. Care work matters, so the question becomes: how do you balance it with creative work?

> YOUR CREATIVE WORK THRIVES WHEN YOU CONSCIOUSLY CHOOSE HOW YOU TAKE ON CAREGIVER TASKS AND WHEN YOU SPEND SOME OF YOUR CAREGIVER ENERGY NURTURING YOURSELF.

Consider What You Carry

One day I had to empty out my purse because there were crumbs at the bottom. After I evicted the offending crumbs, I surveyed my purse contents, now strewn across the table. My purse was so light in my hand while empty. Instead of simply reloading all the items, I considered each one and asked myself, "Do I really need to carry this?" In considering, I discovered an entire category of items which I only carried in case someone else might need them. I carried a constant burden on the off chance someone might need an adhesive bandage…or a note pad…or an extra pen.

When you are a caregiver, the consequences of not being prepared tend to land on you. I developed the habit of carrying extra items during the time when most of my departures from the house meant taking young children with me. Preparedness was survival, so I carried extra stuff "just in case." But that is not the shape of my caregiving anymore. I don't need to carry all the resources to instantly have them on hand. Many of the purposes of preparedness can be served by keeping a first aid kit in my car without me having to carry the weight. The contents of my purse were out of sync with my current needs.

In deciding what to put back into my purse and what to carry as a daily burden, I considered each item. If the result of not having it was of low consequence, I left it out. This same principle can be applied to all your caretaking tasks. Think about what you assign to yourself. Where is the burden not worth the benefit? Giving up extra burdens will give you more energy for your creative work.

The Emotions of Care Work

In the term "care work," the word "care" has two implied meanings. One is tending to the tasks necessary to assist someone else. The second is the emotional connection you feel toward the object of your assistance. Being an emotionally detached caregiver is possible, but unusual. Even paid professional care workers usually form some emotional relationship to the person or thing they're tending.

Once emotions are engaged, you rejoice when the object of your care thrives, and you grieve when they don't. As discussed in Chapter 7, *Managing Mental Load*, the emotions attached to your tasks cause those tasks to take up more space in your brain. When you pay attention to the emotional burden of your caretaking, you are more able to corral those emotions so the creative cost of them lessens. This is particularly necessary when care work includes attached grief. I tackle the impacts of grief specifically in Chapter 22, *Grief is a Creative Process*. More care work includes grief than might be obvious. Clearly, it is grieving to care for someone who is in the process of dying; however, I discovered a surprising amount of grief entangled with the joys and frustrations of raising children.

Unacknowledged emotions cause us to react and shift to their presence even though we don't realize they are there. When you're able to name the emotions attached to your care work, you have a handle to manage those emotions. Then you can begin to arrange space for your creative work alongside the tasks and emotions of care work.

Boundaries in Care Work

There is an additional layer of complexity to boundary setting when the person you need to set boundaries with is dependent on you for crucial emotional or physical support. When one of my children was in elementary school, homework time was always a big battle. Any time we sat down together to do a math worksheet, she would start talking about how lonely she was at school, thus triggering me to be sympathetic instead of making her do math. Other times she would pick a fight with me about how she wished she belonged to a different family, making me feel hurt and upset.

There were several other tactics as well, all designed to activate my emotions and tangle us in some sort of emotional conversation after which I was too tired or felt too sorry for her to make her do math. She avoided a lot of math sheets this way. The boundary I had to set was that no matter what emotional play she made, I would stay neutral, saying something like, "Oh, that sounds hard. We can talk about that once your math sheet is done." Not surprisingly, once the math sheet was done, she skipped off to play and was no longer interested in addressing the emotional crisis.

My homework boundary was internal rather than external. I didn't declare any new rules to my child, nor did I actively attempt to change her behavior; instead, I set my own internal rules around how I would react when she tried to use emotional manipulation to get out of homework. When doing care work, it is important to put boundaries around your emotions. There are times to feel all the feelings and there are times to get things done. This emotional distance can seem heartless, but it is necessary for your long-term ability to care and continue your care work.

Emotional space is particularly important when the person you're caring for is struggling with big emotions: grief, anxiety, anger, or depression. You have to remember that the best way to save someone from drowning is to toss them a rope or a life preserver, not to jump in the pool with them. During the years when I had highly emotional teenagers, I was sometimes all-in on assisting them sort out their big emotions at a moment's notice.

Other times, I took action to make sure they were safe, and then stepped away instead of spending hours as the receptacle of their emotional dump.

If the care work is more mundane than emotional, like round-the-clock diaper changing and feeding of an infant, boundaries may need to be negotiated with other people who also help care for the infant. You have to negotiate who does what care work and when. A baby can't understand your need for fifteen quiet minutes to eat lunch, but another adult can give you those fifteen minutes by caring for the baby. The infant and toddler stages of parenting are so intense they build habits and responses in parental brains that need to be unpacked and re-wired later. You have to jump responsively for your toddler, but an older child or teenager can (and should) be able to wait fifteen minutes while you eat your lunch. One of the tasks of parenting is to learn when it is time to stop jumping in to answer needs and instead step back to let kids cope with their own crises.

One of the big challenges of care work is that any time you take off has to be assigned to someone else. If there is no one else, then that becomes the first problem to apply your creativity to either by building a network or financing professional help. You may need to spend short-term focused creative energy to find long-term solutions that give you more space and energy for your creative projects. The process of adjusting your life so you have help, money to hire help, or resources to solve problems may absorb most of your creative energy for a time, which can be frustrating or discouraging. But small changes accumulate over time to put you and the person you care for into a better position. Every small change you implement will help create structure that increases the creative space you have overall.

Another important tactic in care work is setting boundaries around your own expectations. If you hope to do work while baby is napping and then baby doesn't nap, feeling resentful is likely. If you weren't counting on the nap, then you can greet the opportunity to create with joy. Planning on interruption allows you to roll with interruption. It helps you dodge the emotional blow of wanting some time to yourself and not getting it. This sort of emotional boundary setting comes with a caution, however. Training yourself to not plan for or create times for your projects is only good when you are coping with an unpredictable agent of chaos you can't bargain with (like a baby or a toddler). If you only ever get creative time when you just happen to find unclaimed minutes, you've bought a ticket to the Land of Depletion. A review of the chapters in the *Energy* section of this book, might help you find the right boundaries and balance.

Disaster Recovery Plans

Your daily plan and the way your day actually turns out can be very similar or wildly different. One of the tasks of a caregiver is to adapt to changes in your plans as they happen. Sometimes the changes only require a little adjusting, while at other times you may face a disaster that derails the whole day (baby didn't sleep, so today is a wash), or whole week (car is in the shop, so all plans need adjusting), or even a whole year (surgery and physical therapy). Some changes are so big, they affect everything that comes afterward (a big diagnosis, getting married, getting divorced).

You can't plan specifically for what will come at you in the future, but you can create systems and structures to give space to adapt to whatever may come. This is where the concept of being your own guest as explored in Chapter 9, *Depletion and Replenishment*, can be critical. When you're already stretched to capacity doing care work, it is important to spend a little bit of your caregiving energy to be kind to your future self. Do you have a spare moment today? You should absolutely use it to do something that gives you respite, but you should also use a tiny portion of it to do something to make your burdens lighter in the future.

Rewards of Care Work

Thus far, this chapter has discussed caregiving as a challenge to be overcome. This framing is both accurate and not necessarily true. Caring for others can be the most rewarding and soul-filling work of your life. It can revitalize you instead of depleting you. If care work is daily and non-stop, however, it can cause you to focus on the work instead of the caring. When your care work feels like a burden, I invite you to go back to some of the activities in Chapter 2, *Priorities*, to reconnect to why you've taken on this care work. Connecting to the reasons behind your care work will help you see it as a positive thing rather than a drain. Transforming your care work into an inflow will give you more energy for the other creative projects you want to do.

Activities

Caregiving Activity 1
Identifying Your Care Work

Purpose: To recognize how much care work you have in your life.

Grab your writing tools and set a timer for about five minutes. Write down all the tasks you do whose purpose is to tend to someone else. You can cluster the tasks into categories such as "parenting" or "elder care." You may also want to include a section for self-care tasks. Remember to include things you may not have previously considered to be caretaker tasks, such as grocery shopping, errands, or home maintenance. Any time you do something so another person doesn't have to, that is care work.

At the end of the time, your list is likely to be large. Spend a few moments free writing about any patterns you see in the list or how the list makes you feel. We'll use this list again later.

Caregiving Activity 2
Putting Stuff Down

Purpose: To examine some of what you've been carrying and make conscious decisions about what to put down or hand off to other people.

Take a look at the list of your caregiving tasks. Pick the one weighing you down the most. Write it on a page and then ask yourself the following questions:

- **What are the consequences if this task is done imperfectly or not done at all?** If the consequences are low and the burden on you is high, then that task is a prime candidate for dropping or handing off.
- **Who else can do this task?** This is a question about whether someone is capable of learning the task, not whether they're already trained and skillful at it. Write down as many names as you can. Some of the people you write down might need training to do the task or do it to your standards. That is fine. Don't forget the possibility of hiring help if finances allow.
- **What are the steps necessary to train a person or hand off this task?** It might be as simple as a conversation asking them to take it on, or it might be an extended training process. If hiring help is under consideration, write down the necessary financial steps to secure funding to pay for the help.
- **What timeline feels reasonable for handing off this task?** Teaching kids to do their own laundry is likely a longer process than asking another adult to handle laundry.
- **What are the short-term, medium-term, and long-term trade-offs in handing off this task?** Given all of the above, consider whether the work necessary to hand off the task is worth it to you. Make sure you consider whether a short-term increase in stress while training someone will provide you with long-term relief.
- **Is handing off this task worth it right now?** It may not be. Sometimes the disruption necessary to hand off a task is bigger than the gain from having it off your list.

Repeat this analysis for as many tasks as needed until you find at least one you can put down or let someone else carry.

Caregiving Activity 3
Defining Your Caretaking Work

Purpose: To consciously set boundaries around some of the care you provide to others.

Look at your list of caregiving tasks and focus on any you have decided not to drop or hand off to others. Pick one to focus on, and then consider the following questions:

- **What is the core purpose of this task, and how does it connect to your priorities?** If you're the emotional support for an elderly parent, that work might serve your priority of being a dutiful child.
- **What aspects of this care work are outside that core priority?** Being emotional support probably shouldn't require you to be on call 24/7.
- **List what is and what is not your job relating to this care work.** Make sure you list things that are not your job. Checking in with your elderly mother twice weekly to listen to whatever she has to say might be part of the job, but perhaps those calls can be scheduled instead of fielding twenty random calls during the week.

When considering what may be outside your job description, I recommend writing things down in strong declarative statements such as "Managing Joe's emotions about Sam's birthday is not my job." The strength and clarity of the wording will help you remember it when Joe comes to you with a big pile of feelings.

Fixing a kid's lunch is your job, but putting the lunch into the backpack is their job. Rescuing them from the consequences of a forgotten lunch is an extra job, and you get to decide whether to take it on.

Chapter 21

Health Challenges and Creativity

My husband Howard wrote and illustrated a daily comic for twenty years without missing a single day. His productivity and dedication were the basis of the publishing business that supported our family of six. Then in early 2020, Howard got sick, and he didn't get better. We eventually gathered the term "Long COVID" to describe the change in his capacity. Before, he was a person who moved fast, and I had to run to keep up. After, he was a person who stopped to catch his breath while ambling in the grocery store. As of this writing, we're four years into this profound shift in our lives, and we're still figuring out how to adjust.

During this same period, I was diagnosed with an autoimmune disorder that required strict dietary changes. We changed from a couple who ran fast, accomplished much, and ate all the delicious food to people who carefully think about how we spend our energy and who read every label before eating the contents. The impact on an individual day doesn't feel like much, but the changes accumulate into a huge shift in how we manage our lives. Part of my personal journey of adaptation has been discovering the huge, compassionate community of people who struggle with disability. I am so grateful for the guidance in how to cope. Much of what I've learned has helpful applications in building structure to support creativity whether you are a person whose health impacts your ability to be creative or not.

YOUR CREATIVE WORK THRIVES WHEN YOU HAVE STRATEGIES TO MANAGE HEALTH CHALLENGES AND THE EMOTIONS THAT COME WITH THOSE CHALLENGES.

Fatigue Management and Spoon Theory

A common visualization for fatigue-based health challenges is called spoon theory. First written by Christine Miserandino for butyoudontlooksick.com, it uses spoons as a unit of measure. Each morning you are issued a certain number of spoons. Each task you complete or decision you make uses up a spoon. When you run out, you can't handle any more that day. This is expressed as "running out of spoons." Chronically ill people don't get many spoons. The average person might get fifty spoons a day, while the chronically ill person might only get three. Additional difficulty comes with some health conditions like Chronic Fatigue Syndrome (CFS) or Post Exertional Malaise (PEM) — Howard has both — where the last spoon of the day is attached to a grenade which blows up the spoon supply for the next week…or month…or year. Even worse, the chronically ill can't always tell which spoon is the last one. Sometimes walking up the stairs uses one spoon, other times three — they don't know until they climb them.

Whether or not you struggle with a too-small spoon supply, your creative projects will benefit if you carefully learn where your limits are so you can make choices about which tasks in your life are worth spending your spoons. Obviously, there is an extra urgency if you've got a spoon grenade. This is where knowledge from the disability community greatly benefited Howard and me. We learned to use fitness trackers and apps designed to help Howard stay away from that exploding spoon. (Howard likes the Visible app and Polar arm band.)

Howard does not like having such a limited capacity for creative projects, but the spoon metaphor has helped us not spend spoons where they aren't needed. We also deploy many of the tactics described in Chapter 9, *Depletion and Replenishment*. The concept of the fast recharge came directly from our efforts to find ways to give Howard more useful work hours per day.

Variable Capacity

In discussing spoon theory, I wrote that the average person gets fifty spoons daily. The picture is actually more complex. No one is guaranteed a certain number of spoons per day. You (and everyone else) have variable capacity. You have days with fewer or more spoons than usual. Your spoon count may fluctuate in a narrow range that is easy to plan for, or you might have much larger fluctuations requiring more adaptation.

An essential component of the creative life Howard and I lead together is that, after we do our separate morning routines, we meet up in the kitchen to make breakfast. This breakfast meeting serves multiple purposes. It is a chance for us to connect and share thoughts we've collected. It allows Howard to make sure I eat a hot and delicious meal rather than just eating cold hummus with a spoon (because that's easy and fits my food restrictions). Watching the way Howard moves while cooking allows me to assess how much he pauses for breath and whether he's thinking clearly. At the end of breakfast, we each state our plan for the day. If Howard is out of breath and brain-foggy, we plan the day and our expectations differently than if he is alert and moving well. On the days when energy is limited, we return to our priorities and make sure that if Howard can only do one thing today, it is the most important thing.

If your life is bounded by having less capacity than you want, and every day requires making choices between priorities, sometimes the only answer is to make sure each important thing gets a turn. Rotate between your top priorities, perhaps assign them days. On Monday house admin tasks come first, Tuesday your creative projects come first, on Wednesday you do errands, etc. Rotation does not solve the problem of too little energy, but it can help make sure your limited energy is spent in a balanced way.

Be very careful when you're tempted to "just push through" and do all the tasks anyway. When you overspend your energy on one day, you borrow from your future self. That debt will come due. You're better served with a process that adjusts today's expectations to today's capacity. Give yourself kindness when you can't do everything you want to be able to do.

Unfortunately, the reality is that sometimes you have no choice but to overspend sometimes, especially when your capacity is limited and life demands are high. I recommend returning to Chapter 9, *Depletion and Replenishment*, to see if any of the tactics there can be applied to your situation. You also have my sympathies. This situation describes my life more often than I want.

Building Interdependence

Living with health challenges often requires interdependence with other people. Unlike co-dependence ("I need you to stay broken and disabled so I can retain my emotionally-important role of helping you"), interdependence is just an extension of a support network. It is using one person's strengths to fill in for the weakness of another. Howard and I cooking together is an excellent example of this. I do most of the fetching, chopping, bending, and lifting. Howard does the innovative thinking necessary to adapt foods to my restricted diet. Between the two of us, we accomplish work that would be difficult for either of us to accomplish alone. This same interdependence extends to the creative business we share. We divide up the creative work according to personal strengths. Then we collaborate to cover the places where disability or lack of skill require extra support.

Interdependence is not only for people who live in your household. You can develop interdependence with your larger community as well. This starts with the "naming what you need" process I discussed in the *Managing Relationships* section of this book. If you need a weekly ride to the grocery store, perhaps you know someone who could use a shopping buddy. If you have household chores, maybe a friend can hang out with you while you fold laundry on Tuesday and then Thursday, you hang out with them while they clean out their fridge. If you need a support group for your particular challenge, perhaps you can find one or start one. There is huge healing power in not being alone with your difficulties. There is even more power when you help ease the difficulties of others.

If you're seeking a framework for developing this sort of community interdependence, the Pods and Pod Mapping Worksheet* created by Mia Mingus is an excellent starting place. This worksheet will help you see what connections you have and will guide you in figuring out how to strengthen those connections or create new ones. I've formed one of the activities at the end of this chapter around this worksheet.

Developing a healthy interdependence requires a lot of communication and honesty about needs. It also requires a willingness to adapt when needs change. As they inevitably do.

Compensating for Emotions

The emotional toll of daily health challenges and disabilities can be high. Howard and I grieve the changes in our lives. Sometimes there are days where the grief takes over time I'd intended to use for a creative project. Grief has a creative cost. I explore that cost more fully in Chapter 22, *Grief is a Creative Process*.

If you have health challenges, feelings about those challenges can be part of what you need to cope with daily. You may need support in facing and processing those emotions. This emotional support may be part of the interdependence you build with others. Mental health professionals and support groups with expertise in

* Mia Mingus created the worksheet for the BATJC (https://batjc.org/files/Pods-Pod-Mapping-Worksheet.pdf

situations like yours could be resources to you. Frequently, the emotions about our health challenges are more an impediment to our creative work than the challenges themselves.

If you don't face daily health challenges, you need to understand that feelings about life circumstances are highly individual. Do not assume because two people share the same visible circumstance, their inward feelings must be the same. The life-long wheelchair user is going to have a very different emotional relationship to their mobility tool than someone who has recently acquired a need for a wheelchair. The best way to find out how someone feels about their challenges is to ask them. Note: this doesn't mean you should quiz people on the street. Even a friend might not be willing to open up the interior of their emotional experience to you.

Physical Spaces Revisited

When Howard started using a cane, we attached a strong magnet to the cane and installed metal plates all over the house so that wherever Howard went, he had a place to "dock" his cane if he needed both hands free. We also rearranged the kitchen to optimize movement efficiency. You can do something similar. Look at your spaces and think about how you can make life easier. Can you store the things you need closer to where you need them? Can you put a stool in the kitchen so you can sit while cooking? Can you spend one day's spoons on chopping ingredients so you have less chopping to do on the following days?

When energy is limited, the effort necessary to reconfigure your physical spaces may be expensive. We spent six months figuring out how to rig a reclined workstation that allowed Howard to have ready access to his drawing tools without needing to leave his chair. The creative cost was high, with Howard spending more than half his energy tinkering on his workspace instead of actually working. But having the reclined workspace expanded the amount of work Howard was able to do each day. Spending energy refining your spaces can give back time and energy for your creative projects. I recommend going through Chapter 11, *Your Physical Space*, with an eye toward arranging your surroundings for your health challenges.

When considering how to change your physical space to adapt for health challenges, pay attention to clutter. Every object you own requires care, attention, and space. Many of those objects bring you joy and thus are worth the effort you spend on them. But odds are good you have a lot of extra objects in your life that you don't need and which may be burdening you with caretaking chores. Getting rid of extra stuff may make room for your creative projects both physically and through the reclaimed energy of no longer having to track and store those items. Decluttering takes energy, but the result is a more functional space for your creative projects.

Food Planning and Proactive Self-Care

When you're dealing with health challenges, the consequences of missed meals may be higher for you than others. This is also true about skipped self-care. You need to get enough sleep, do your physical therapy, take naps, eat regularly, take your medicines, and schedule appointments. The burden of this life admin creates mental load and reduces the creative energy you have available for your projects. Remember: all of this burden is maintenance to keep you functional. If you are not functional, you cannot create anything. So, frustrating though it may be, pro-active self-care and food planning are part of the structure you need to make space for your creative projects.

When my kids were little, dinnertime was exhausting. Everyone was cranky and tired, including me. I discovered that planning a week's worth of dinner in advance really helped me on a daily basis because I had already done the thinking and shopping. I could just follow my own instructions. Similar patterns are helpful now when dealing with the overlap of Howard's disabilities and my dietary restrictions. We use mornings when we have focus and energy to plan ahead for food in the afternoon and evening when we know we'll be tired. This "plan ahead" also affects our shopping. Sometimes instead of planning ahead with our own chopping, for example, we buy pre-chopped items.

We also spend money on kitchen devices that will save physical exertion and effort. A food processor and a pressure cooker have significantly reduced the amount of time Howard spends standing while cooking. You may want to look at your particular challenge and then search to see if there are devices designed to make that challenge easier.

The Narrative of Your Challenges

At a recent group lunch, a friend leaned over and asked quietly, "How is Howard doing? Is he getting any better?" Some form of this question gets asked of both Howard and me in a lot of different contexts. In that moment, we have to decide whether to go with the polite answer which quickly allows us to change the topic to something else, or to open up the topic of our life challenges and the emotions we carry about them.

Chronic conditions are hard for people to understand if they haven't lived with them. Howard is not getting better, not in the way my friend's question asks. Sometimes we find things that increase his ability to work, other times his capacities decline. New science and treatments could change this reality, but they haven't yet. We're more able to focus on our creative work if we accept things as they are instead of waiting for them to return to what they were. This internal acceptance of our situation does not make it easier to know how to answer kind questions. For that, I rely on pre-planned scripts. Howard's current preferred answer is, "We're coping better. Thank you for asking."

Pre-planned scripts for how you'll answer common inquiries can help you avoid the moment when a kind question opens a pile of emotions you don't want to spill in public. When I'm going out to eat with friends, the public negotiation with the waiter about which menu items contain what allergens often leads to people asking polite questions about my diet. Discussions of my medical challenges have the potential to spill emotions, so I pre-plan what I'll order before I get there. Currently, my diet restrictions are so severe, it usually means a soda, and me saying, "Oh, I ate before I came. I'm here for the company, not the food." Then, I immediately ask my friends a question so we can skip the conversation where I have to explain my diet restrictions and listen to others react.

There is a complex calculus around what level of information about your medical challenges to give to what person in what venues. Shutting everyone out is not good for you. You need people to understand your life and challenges. But that doesn't mean you want to spill everything to anyone who asks. So, pick your time, place, and the person to whom you're willing to share deeply. For the rest, rehearsed, socially acceptable answers let you change the subject to something you want to talk about.

The Unexpected Gifts

Neither Howard nor I would have chosen our health challenges if given the option to refuse them. Yet, adapting to them taught us skills we would not otherwise have learned. Learning how to work slow has given us a different relationship to our lives and the work we do. We have more resilience and persistence than our younger selves could have mustered. All of this has shaped and deepened our creative work. We have learned how to see the gifts in hard circumstances. To be honest, most days I don't feel particularly grateful for our health challenges, but on the days I do, I feel peaceful and more able to turn my focus to my creative projects.

If you have health challenges, finding your way to gratitude and acceptance creates more space for your creative projects. This can start with the surface level practices of "looking on the bright side" or "finding the silver lining." You can even deploy a notebook as you've done in prior chapters to catch the things you're grateful for and the ways that your challenges teach you. Noting these observations teaches your mind to notice more of them. Health challenges often come with attached grief, so you may have some emotional processing to do before you're able to see any benefit from your challenges. Benefits and learning also accumulate over time. When your challenge is new, you may not have learned anything from it yet.

Activities

Health Challenges Activity 1
The Pod Mapping Worksheet

Purpose: To take a close look at the current state of your network so you can make decisions about how to develop your interdependence.

Print out a copy of the pod-mapping worksheet below or use a blank piece of paper and draw your own circles. Decide what aspect of your interconnectedness you want to examine in your worksheet. I recommend the following maps as starting places:

- Physical support
- Financial support
- Emergency support (fire, weather event, power outage)
- Emotional support
- Creative work support

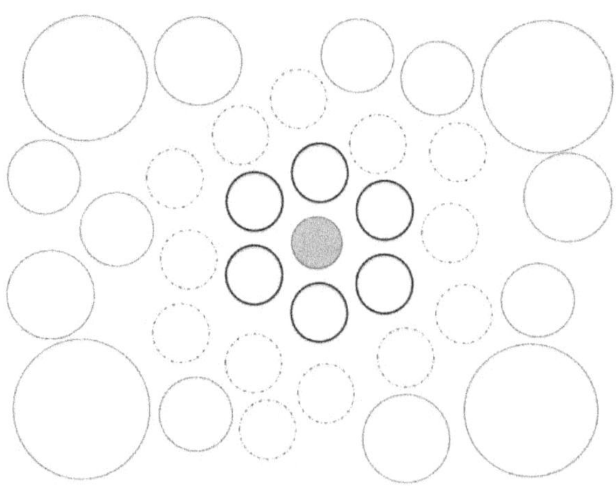

The central circle is you. Write your own name.

The bold circles are the people you can count on to always pick up your call, show up for you, or answer your need at a moment's notice. Write individual names of specific people rather than groups like "my church congregation."

The dotted line circles are people who could be in the bold circle, but with whom you need to adjust your relationship to make that happen.

The larger circles around the edges are where you put groups or organizations that you can consider resources. This is where you put your church congregation or social group.*

Health Challenges Activity 2
Finding Adaptive Tools

Purpose: To discover adaptive tools that will help you manage your health in ways that reduce the creative cost.

Search the internet using the term "adaptive tools for [your diagnosis or symptoms]." Write down a list of all of the suggested tools, even ones you don't want to use. For any of the tools you don't want, consider doing a free write on why you resist that tool. Is it because you're having an emotional reaction to using the tool or is it because deploying that tool would require significant reconfiguration of your spaces (e.g., a wheelchair might require home remodeling)?

Pick one tool you're willing to try out and can afford. Assign yourself a set period of time to try it out, then evaluate whether it helped or not.

* "Pod Mapping Worksheet" is a resource belonging to the BATJC and written by Mia Mingus. (https://batjc.org/files/Pods-Pod-Mapping-Worksheet.pdf) It is used here via the Creative Commons Share Alike license. I've made slight changes to focus and wording in describing how to use this worksheet. Some of those changes were influenced by "Pod Mapping for Mutual Aid" by Rebel Sydney Black. (https://docs.google.com/document/d/1-QfMn1DE6ymhKZMpXN1LQvD6Sy_HSnnCK6gTO7ZLFrE/mobilebasic)

Health Challenges Activity 3
Physical Space Redux

Purpose: To revisit the activities in Chapter 11 with an eye to specifically addressing challenges related to your health.

Review the activities in Chapter 11, *Your Physical Space*, and re-do them while thinking specifically about how you can optimize for variable capacity, efficiency of movement, or any other aspects of health challenges covered in this chapter.

Chapter 22

Grief is a Creative Process

I always thought I would create more if I had more time, but the pandemic shutdowns of spring and summer 2020 proved me wrong. All my obligations were cancelled and the result was not productivity. In September of that year, I helped run an online social event for writers. Prior versions of these events had been full of talk about worldbuilding, characters, or plots. This time we talked about our changed lives, and we shared frustration with how little we were getting done. It became clear to me we were all grieving — not a single loss, but a multitude of losses, both big and small. We grieved for events canceled, for the haircuts we wished we could get, for all the deaths, for the separation from loved ones, and for the lives we used to have. We talked for hours at that online social and only scratched the surface of what we carried.

Yet, in the week following, I could write again. It astonished me, and I had to pause to understand it. Why had grieving stopped me from creating? Why did sharing and commiserating about the grief make creating possible again?

To understand, I had to think back to an earlier encounter with grief. Two decades before the pandemic I had radiation therapy to eliminate a non-cancerous tumor in my neck. It was six weeks of daily treatments designed to kill a batch of rogue cells without killing me. The treatments made eating difficult, and I had visible radiation burns before the end. By the time the course was done, I was eager to move on with my life. I shoved all of those experiences and my feelings about them to the back of my mind like boxes in the back of an attic. But every year, as I approached the anniversary of my treatments, I became depressed, struggling to meet the demands of my life.

By trying to move past the emotions and grief of my medical experience, what I'd actually done was preserve those emotions and griefs, allowing them to leak and cause annual problems. Seven years after the radiation, I opened up those mental boxes and began to process my feelings through writing. I wrote out all my experiences and felt what I'd been avoiding. It was a lot of words. When I was done, I put the writing away where I would not accidentally see it.

The year after that, I was not depressed on the anniversary. Instead of carrying boxes of grief that required effort to ignore and contain, I had learned and grown from that grief, dispelling much of its power over me. I no longer have seasonal depression stealing my energy away from my creative projects. In fact, that time of the year has become one where everything feels quieter, and I have more focus for my creative projects.

That story of my recovery from medical trauma is simple and straightforward: I had an event, I wrote about the event to process it, then I was all better. The reality, however, was more tangled. Although I no longer have the annual depression, I still have physical and emotional scarring from that event. In addition, spending time to sort and process grief came with a creative cost. During the time I wrote to process my emotions about radiation therapy, I did not have energy for other creative work. This is because grief is a creative process. It is the process by which you deconstruct what was and find the pieces to build what comes next.

When I wrote about radiation therapy, I was taking a close look at everything that happened to me. I was also incorporating thoughts and lessons I would carry forward. While I was talking with those other writers during the pandemic, I was doing the same thing: feeling my grief, sharing it, hearing other perspectives on it, and then carrying it differently.

Grief is beautiful and necessary. It is a transformative gift you don't want to receive. But if you grow with it, learn from it, and incorporate its lessons into your life, you will become stronger and better than you could otherwise be.

Grief sticks around for a long time and pops up unexpectedly. You don't want your creative work to always wait on grief, so you need to find ways to work even when you're in the middle of it.

YOUR CREATIVE WORK THRIVES WHEN YOU UNDERSTAND THE QUALITIES AND IMPACTS OF GRIEF AND DEPLOY TOOLS TO COPE WITH GRIEF AND PROCESS IT.

Qualities of Grief

Grief Accumulates and Is Patient

You can't outrun or outwait grief. You can't hunker down and expect it to pass while you remain safe and untouched. I tried with my radiation therapy experience and ended up annually depressed. Grief accumulates and ambushes you in unexpected moments. The only way to dispel grief is to be open to the feeling of it. You have to cry and rage and despair. Or hide and heal. You have to let it permeate who you are and slop over into places you're not sure it belongs. You have to process it in a way that works for *you* the way writing worked for me. When you process, the grief becomes part of the fabric of who you are, woven in until it isn't really grief anymore. Instead, it becomes part of how you move forward in the world.

An accumulation of small, unprocessed griefs can be as disruptive to creativity as one giant grief, which was an element of the profound effect the pandemic had on so many creative people. This sort of accumulation can clog up the creative aquifers and flows, as discussed in Chapter 9, *Depletion and Replenishment*. When the grief is small, sometimes you may not even realize you're carrying it around. It might hide under secondary emotions like anger or avoidance. I once found myself crying at the movie trailer for *Annie*. (I couldn't believe that the sun would come out tomorrow.) Tracing the emotion back to its source helped me see I was struggling and depressed. I'd been too busy to notice. So, when you're struggling to create, it is always a good idea to pay attention to the possibility you're carrying unacknowledged grief.

Grief Is Non-Proportional

When discussing grief, it is easy to focus on the big losses that transform your life. But it is possible for a big event to leave you untouched and a small one to break you completely. Especially if a small event taps into a large grief you've kept contained — all of that emotion comes pouring out.

Recently, I had a big cry that derailed my whole day, and it happened because of cheese. Cheese is not on the list of big losses people think of when they contemplate grief. In my particular case, however, the small trigger (cheese I could not eat because of a medically mandated diet) opened up a big reservoir of accumulated emotion. I cried not because of the cheese, but because of the loss of something I loved and, furthermore, because the medical testing I was undergoing stirred up my old medical trauma from my radiation therapy. Grief both old and new gushed out through the small hole in my day made by cheese. It is not the size of the incident or the trigger, but the size of the emotion under the surface that determines our reactions.

If you discover yourself having big reactions to small things, recognize you likely have unprocessed grief affecting your emotional state. This can also affect your ability to do your creative projects. It was two days after my cry over cheese before I had energy and stability enough to return to my creative projects.

Another emotional consequence of grief can be a lack of ability to feel. In order to protect you from sadness, your mind encapsulates all emotion, keeping it far from you. This self-protection can leave you with a very small reaction to even large life events. A consequence of this disconnection from emotion can be disconnection from your creative projects.

Learning how grief and emotion flow through you is vital for being able to make space in your life for creative projects.

Grief Is Messy and Out of Sync

Sometimes, grief processing is out of sync with where you think it should be. I was certain I'd fully processed my trauma over radiation therapy, until I cried over cheese and realized I still held pockets of unreasonable fear even twenty years later. This out of sync processing is particularly true for people who set emotion aside to get stuff done or to handle a crisis. Be kind to yourself when your grief is messy. If you can, extend that kindness to others when they are emotional or reactive in ways you can't understand. It is safe to assume that everyone you meet is grieving something, and perhaps their situation has unlocked an out of sync emotion.

Grief Has Patterns and Cycles

My seasonal depression is one example of how grief can manifest in a recurring cycle. Mine was tied to the season of the year, but grief can also be tied to locations or events. If your grief is long-lasting, it may develop rhythms and patterns for when it is stronger or weaker. Seeing the patterns helps you plan for and navigate around them.

The patterns of your grief may provide clues to help you address and resolve emotions. Even if you can't resolve the emotions, knowing when they're likely to surface can help you plan around those emotions. In much the same way we plan for the weather when going outdoors, you can build your life so your creative projects have shelter from the emotional weather. If you know you always get depressed near the anniversary of a death, try to schedule your creative work to allow yourself down time during that period.

Grief Is Chemical

There are measurable changes in brain chemistry for people who are grieving. When coping with grief, your brain does not function in ways you've been accustomed to. You'll have lower capacity for decision making. You might feel foggy or indecisive. The changes in chemistry may affect your memory as well. This alters your responses to everything around you, including your creative projects.

In hindsight, I can see this is what happened during those pandemic shutdowns. I was running in emergency mode, which changed how I was able to engage with creative work. The changed brain chemistry of grief can slide into long-term chemical depression or anxiety. I recommend seeking out professional help from mental health experts if you are trying to untangle grief that is complex or persistent in your life.

Tools for Grief

Having described why grief can cause very real challenges for your creative projects, I'd like to give you some tools for dealing with those challenges.

Name Your Grief

Names have power. When you look squarely at the grief you carry and name it specifically, that can help you begin to process it. Naming your grief attaches a handle to it. A handle on a pan lets you manage something that would hurt you if you touched it directly. A handle on an unwieldy suitcase gives you the means to haul it where you need it. A handle on a piano is not going to let you move it around easily, but it still provides some leverage for shifting it. You definitely want a handle on your grief. Naming it can give you that.

An example of naming grief: on the day I cried over cheese, once I was done crying, I was able to see how nonproportional my response was. I sat down to free write all my thoughts about cheese and sadness. At the end, I summarized my writing into statements. I ended up with three:

- "Coping with medical issues is scary because I lack control."
- "I am grieving the accumulated weight of not being able to have small things that brought me joy."
- "I am grieving the difficulties of living with a restricted diet."

After sitting with those statements, I summarized further to give a simple two-word name that encapsulated all of it: "food sadness." This is clearly an oversimplification of all my complicated feelings and thoughts. But it gave me a handle. I told my husband Howard all my feelings, the statements, and the name of my grief. Afterwards, on any given day, I could alert him to how I was feeling by simply saying, "I'm having a bit of food sadness today." Because he knew the context, he was able to give me kindness and support.

Having the name gives me a way to talk about and live with my grief daily. With a handle, I'm better able to manage it so I can get other work done.

Seek Resources

Whatever your grief is, you don't have to tough it out alone. You can find help in the form of other people or in the tools other people supply. Seeking help to navigate your grief might look like:

- **Research.** Someone else has been through it before or is going through it right now. Many of those people have created resources that can help you. There may be books, websites, or films that specifically address experiences like yours.
- **Therapy.** There is likely a therapist or counselor who specializes in what you're going through.
- **Support Groups.** You can seek a support group with other people who are going through the same thing.
- **Cathartic Fiction.** There is a reason why break-up movies, and terminal illness movies are popular. Fiction can help us access the feelings we stowed away for our own survival. Note: Approach this one with caution. If your feelings are too raw, you may not be ready for catharsis. Also, maybe connect with a friend who can catch you emotionally and, if needed, help you process.
- **Conscious Hiding.** Grant yourself grace to hide from your grief if you need to. We all need respite from big feelings. Hiding is a healing impulse. Sometimes, we need to NOT

think about our sadness and just feel better for a while. While hiding feels good in the short term, know, though, you can't stay hidden forever. As I said earlier, you can't outwait grief.

Conscious Release of Emotion

When people talk about grief, they often use terms such as "bottled up" or "walled off." This encapsulation of grief is sometimes necessary to keep functioning despite overwhelming emotion. However, the persistence of this containment can lead to disconnection from your feelings, even the good ones. That, in turn, can separate you from your creative projects. The other drawback is that when grief is contained in this way, it is also preserved. If we continue to accumulate grief in this fashion, the internal pressure will eventually breach containment, often not in the places we would want or in ways we would choose. This is what happened with my experience of radiation therapy. My containment preserved the emotions and trapped some lovely memories along with the hard ones. In addition to preserving, my containment leaked, causing my annual depression. I rediscovered the good memories as I unpacked the hard ones.

When you spend effort to contain grief instead of processing it, you have to keep spending that energy until you do the processing. It is like a monthly subscription for a thing you don't want. The energy could be spent on could be spent on other things, like your creative projects.

In order to process your grief, you have to open that containment. Simply sitting with your feelings often leads to stewing in the feelings instead of processing and transforming them. A guide like a therapist, book, or support group might help you open containment safely.

Processing emotion does not always have to take you away from creativity. In fact, many creative activities like collage, painting, drawing, writing, or dance can help you connect with what you are feeling. What you create in these moments is frequently not for public consumption. It is for you and your own healing.

Exert Some Control

The pandemic conversation showed me that even though few of us were working on the creative projects in the way we wanted, most of us had picked up some other pursuit. Some were baking bread and tending plants. I blogged and created hand-tracked charts of pandemic case numbers. It wasn't that creativity vanished, only that our creative energy flowed elsewhere.

When faced with something uncontrollable, like a pandemic or grief, you may turn to something simple you can control. These side projects are good. They get creativity flowing again, and that eventually brings you back to your projects.

Befriend Your Grief

Grief hurts. Hurting is unpleasant. So, it is a natural impulse to treat the hurt like an enemy intrusion, something to push back or reject. If, instead, you think of hurt as a part of yourself, an indicator light giving you information, you can stop wasting energy on defending against the hurt. The pain of grief tells you that you have been injured and need to heal. Understanding your grief and the purpose it serves helps you create ways to move forward with it. It helps you undertake the necessary process of creating what comes next.

Grief brings gifts. Sometimes the gift is, "Well, I've learned I'm strong enough to survive that." You can also gain self-realization, personal transformation, lovely moments, and kindness from others. When you're entering the early stages or are mired in the middle of grief, it is often difficult or impossible to see or appreciate what is gained from that particular grief. But if you are patient, something good usually results from the transformation inherent in grief.

Creativity Will Not Abandon You

No matter what grief you carry or what pain comes to you, trust that your innate creative heart will not abandon you while you deal with other things. I saw some of this during the pandemic. While almost all of my writer friends found themselves struggling to write, creativity burst out in other ways. Many of them took up baking or gardening or photography. When life calmed down and they returned to writing, their side adventure into other creative pursuits informed what they wrote.

Other of my writer friends did not take up new hobbies. They went into a hibernation of binge-watching TV and other distractions. They, too, have found their way back to creative work, just on a different road. That binge watch also informed their creative projects when they found their new paths.

The natural state of humans is to create. If you are not creating, you are probably hurting or healing in some way. When you are in the midst of grief, your creative energy may be fully absorbed in processing your changed life and grief. Let go of the guilt and anxiety over the creative work that got superseded by processing how to live in a changed world. It is okay if your project lays idle for a time. Your creative work will be there when you are ready to return to it. The experience you have will expand and improve the creative project you eventually do.

Activities

Grief Activity 1
Name Your Grief

Purpose: To uncover griefs you may have hidden from yourself and name them.

Sit down with writing tools and ponder the question: "What am I sad about right now?" Free write for as long as you need to, but I recommend giving yourself a minimum of five minutes to make sure you really consider the question. Since grief often hides behind secondary emotions, you may find it useful to repeat the activity, asking yourself, "What am I angry about right now?" and "What feels hopeless right now?"

At the end of your free write, look at what you have uncovered. See if you can summarize your writing into a sentence or two. (An example is the way I summarized my sadness over cheese earlier in this chapter: "I am grieving the accumulated weight of not being able to have small things that brought me joy." Or "I am grieving the difficulties of living with a restricted diet."

Then give your grief a 1-3 word name. (I called my grief over food "food sadness" so I could tell people things like, "I'm having a bit of food sadness today.")

Grief Activity 2
Find Resources for Your Grief

Purpose: To consciously seek out resources to help process your particular grief.

Pull out writing tools and pick a grief you want to consciously address. Write it down on one side of your page. On the other, brainstorm resources or ideas that could help you face and process this grief. Write down all the ideas, even if some are not feasible because of time, energy, or money constraints. Feel free to use the internet, library, or interpersonal connections to generate more ideas.

Then, get practical. Of your listed ideas, which one feels the most possible and matches your inclination and capacity? If you struggle with massive social anxiety, then an in-person support group may not be a good fit for you, but an online group where you can lurk and learn without being perceived might be great. Plan to implement that resource in the near future.

After you've done it, come back and reflect on how it went.

Grief Activity 3
The Gifts of Your Grief

Purpose: To focus on the gifts that grief has brought you. Start with an old grief (as you will have more perspective) before moving into current grief.

Sit down with paper and think about an old grief — one from which you have mostly recovered. Free write about what you learned or gained from having that grief. It is fine if the answer is something like “I learned I could survive.”

Repeat with more recent griefs. (You may want to take breaks in between, so you don’t overwhelm yourself.) The repetition teaches you how to look for the hard, hidden gifts. Do not worry if you can’t come up with anything for fresher griefs. It often requires perspective before we can see the gifts. If you’re completely stumped, see if you can find someone willing to help you think it through. Make sure that person is in a stable place, and the effort won’t breach their own containment on grief, particularly if they share the same grief.

Grief Activity 4
Reconnect to Your Work

Purpose: To refocus your attention on the creative work you want to be doing and reconnect with it.

Write a note to your creativity about the things you are not doing. You could write to your creative self, or to the specific book, painting, or garden you aren’t working on, or to a character from the stories you haven’t managed to tell yet. Whatever you pick, tell it you miss it and what you miss about it. For a bonus round, write the note your project sends back to you.

Chapter 23

When Creative Work Hurts

In the final years of our elderly kitty's life, she developed kidney disease. We discovered this because there was a day when we could not find her, and unlike her usual habits, she did not come when called. We eventually found her hiding under a bush in the corner of the garden. Medical treatment returned her to health, and we had several more good years with her after that day, but had we not found her, the disease would have killed her in only a day or two. Hiding was not in her best interest, but my cat was faced with pain she couldn't understand, and instinct told her to hide in a place that felt safe.

Like my cat, you have an entire instinctual section of the brain devoted to helping you keep yourself safe from things that might hurt you. The instinct to turn away and hide when faced with pain is strong, so you avoid things that might cause pain or remind you of past pain. Often this avoidance happens subconsciously. You might clean instead of writing for example. This same avoidance of pain can cause you to do things like avoid a hobby you once loved because you were hurt by people in the hobby group. This self-protective instinct can be a problem because creativity requires a certain amount of vulnerability. You have to be willing to risk being hurt. If you've been hurt in the past your self-protective instincts may push you away from your creative work in an attempt to protect you from future hurt.

Unlike my cat, you are capable of understanding your pain and choosing how to respond to it. You're able to prevent the protective instincts from causing you to hide in the bushes instead of seeking care.

YOUR CREATIVE WORK THRIVES WHEN YOU UNDERSTAND YOUR HURT AND TAKE THE TIME TO HEAL FROM IT.

Complex Injury and Simple Injury

Sometimes, when we're injured, we know precisely when and how it happened, like a twisted ankle. Other times the cause is unclear, like a shoulder where the ache increases over time. Both injuries are fairly straightforward, and the path to healing is simple. You have to change how you use the affected area until your body has time to heal. (Note: simple is not the same as easy. Ask anyone who has been prescribed "rest" to aid healing.) Other injuries are far more complex to diagnose or heal from. Some injuries require surgery or extensive therapy to restore function. Emotional or mental traumas work similarly to physical traumas. Some are complex and some are simple.

Suffering from an emotional or mental hurt can change your behavior around your creative projects, sometimes without you consciously realizing it. Any time you have a big emotional reaction to something, particularly if the reaction is out of scale with your usual reactions, it is probably an indicator you have an injury that needs healing.

Hurt Feelings Are Injuries

When approaching an emotional injury, it is important not to minimize it. Hurt feelings are a real injury, whether a momentary hurt that is easy to shake off or a complex hurt that activates and aggravates existing injuries. The size of the injury doesn't change the fact of the injury. Society tends to minimize hurt feelings: you should "just get over them." While it's true you may need to put those hurt feelings aside for a time to accomplish tasks, you still have to heal from the hurt. If you don't heal, hurt can accumulate and worsen.

Taking Control of Healing

The existence of emotional injury can sap creative energy as you try to work around and adapt for the hurt. This is why doing the work to help yourself heal can help you re-focus on your creative projects. Like physical injuries, the path toward healing an emotional, mental, or creative injury depends on the type of injury. Sometimes, you need rest; other times, you need a more significant intervention analogous to surgery. Medical providers are taught techniques to manage patients with trauma. They are taught to create safety, build trust, and give choices. Do the same for yourself when you're trying to heal.

- Create safety. This might look like finding a place to be alone so you're comfortable crying. Or you might create safety by seeking out a person who will listen without judgment.
- Build trust. Every time you survive and grow after being hurt, you learn hurt is survivable. Until you trust you can survive, you may need to use conscious decisions and reminders to help you face the hurt instead of defaulting to instinctive reactions (like hiding).
- Give Choices. When you are consciously addressing your hurts, you will feel more in control of the process if you claim your choices. Try forming these choices into declarative statements. "I choose to be kind to this person even though they have hurt me." Or "I choose to no longer associate with this person because they have not acknowledged or apologized for the harm they have done." Or "I will find a time to confront this person with the fact their actions have hurt me."

If you let someone know their actions hurt your feelings and they don't apologize or repair, you might need to set a protective boundary between that person and your feelings.

Protective Boundaries

An everyday example of a feelings boundary is between co-workers in a workplace. By mutual consent, large portions of conversations are about your shared work and collaboration, not about your personal lives or feelings. This division is important even if you are friends with your co-workers. (Most of my work relationships are blended with friend relationships.) Work space is not feelings space. There are two aspects to this feelings boundary, managing your own feelings and managing the feelings of others.

When managing the feelings of others, this sort of boundary can be as simple as re-directing the conversation back to work topics, and, if the person is a friend and you're open to hearing about it after work, offering that option. You are not required to hear about it after work, or at all. Being a person who responds with kindness and care to the feelings of others is a good thing, but don't allow the feelings of others to pull you off course or overwrite your feelings and needs. Just because someone has big feelings in front of you doesn't mean it is your job to resolve them. If someone else's feelings regularly disrupt your creative projects, there is a problem, and boundaries are necessary to correct it.

When managing your own feelings, it is important to prevent your emotional responses from intruding on others inappropriately. In order to accomplish this, it is critical for you to know when, where, and with whom you can vent your feelings. You may have different places and people depending on what emotions you need to process. A lot of people who overshare inappropriately do so because they don't have a defined space where those feelings are fully allowed. If someone tells you your feelings are not their job, that rebuff can really sting, especially if you have a friendship with them. The rebuff can be as direct as mocking or as subtle as changing the subject. It is important to respect that rebuff and take your feelings elsewhere.

If you are in a situation where your feelings are repeatedly hurt, whether from carelessness, malice, or simply because you have an active wound that keeps getting bumped, then you might need to find a way to leave that situation. Leaving can be hard if the "situation" is a community or intertwined with the creative work that you love. I've had to step back from people and events that were hurting me. Sometimes, that departure was a permanent divergence; other times, I have been able to sort myself, untangle the feelings, heal, and then reconnect.

The Shame Spiral

If you have high expectations for yourself and then don't meet those expectations, you may discover yourself in a shame spiral. The spiral looks like this:

- **Failure.** Fail at an intended action.
- **Shame.** Feel bad for failing.
- **Avoid.** Hide from feeling bad.
- **Repeat.** Each repetition feels worse.

If the action you fail at is your creative project, this spiral can lead you to avoid the project for long periods even extending to years or decades. The shame spiral is never helpful. There are several places where you can challenge the spiral and redirect yourself into a better framing of what is happening.

Examine whether imposter syndrome, anxiety, or self-doubt are impacting your perceptions of failure. You may feel like you failed at something when you haven't. The first defense against the shame spiral is to do a reality check on whether or not your perceptions of failure are accurate. Re-reading Chapter 18, Cultivating Confidence, may help with this. You can also go to someone in your support network and ask them if they'll listen to you talk through your perceived failures and give you an objective opinion. You want someone who will listen as you sort and will only try to problem solve if invited to do so.

Another place to disrupt the spiral is to lean into the shame instead of trying to flee from it. You failed at something, and you feel bad about it. Why do you feel bad? Is this failure contained to the task you failed at, or does it connect to larger priorities and insecurities in your life? If you failed to meet a deadline, it is your shame only that you let other people down in this case, or does it become emblematic of who you are as a whole person? If the latter, why does one incident make you feel bad about your whole existence? Facing shame in this way may help you uncover deep fears and insecurities which you now have the opportunity to address. It is not an easy or comfortable process, but in the long run healing these insecurities can help you avoid shame spirals and let you focus more on your projects.

The third place you can interrupt the spiral is by working on the shame itself, by granting yourself grace for your failures. Failures are data, not a referendum on your value as human being. You can recognize you failed without telling yourself a story about how that failure makes you awful. When you do this, you can skip the shame spiral and decide how to move forward in a way that prevents you from repeating the failure.

Jealousy Comes from Depletion

I have many brilliant and successful friends. I am so happy for their triumphs. … most of the time. Occasionally, when I hear about someone else's success, I feel jealous. Professional jealousy can happen to anyone; feeling jealous does not make you a bad person. It usually means the person you feel jealous of has something that you lack and you're being reminded of that lack by their success. The solution is not to tear down the other person. Your jealousy isn't really about them; it is about your lack or depletion. When I hear about a friend's book deal and am jealous, if I focus on the feeling, I can recognize I am currently feeling financially strained and wish I had a deal that would pay me money. Hearing about the exact same deal when I'm not feeling financially stressed would not spark any jealousy because I have what I need and can simply be happy for my friend.

When you feel jealous, it is time to seek what depletion is the source of that feeling. It is also a moment to choose carefully when and with whom you vent those feelings. Your feelings are valid and need to be processed. Just remember that jealous feelings are like knives, and if not handled with care, they can cut people, starting with you.

Reclaiming Joy from Hurt

When you are hurting, the pain can absorb all of your attention and drive all of your actions. You might become like my cat, acting on instinct when she hid from people who could help her. One of the ways you can change your experience of hurt and help yourself toward healing is to consciously reach for and claim joy. Claiming joy can look like:

- When you are struggling with shame spirals, remembering that you feel bad because you want to be good at something you love. Connecting with that love can help you skip the shame and get back to the thing you want to be good at doing.
- When you have to leave a situation or relationship for your peace and healing, trying to separate the parts you love and carrying them to a new place instead of abandoning everything.
- When you are setting boundaries, making space for joy to thrive. Give yourself time to do things for the joy of them whether or not they help you achieve goals or progress.
- When you are beset by jealousy, taking time to consciously feel joy for your friend's success. When you connect with that joy, it will quiet the harder feelings.
- When you are healing, noticing the small gains. You may not be where you want to be, but focusing on the good can help you feel more joy in the progress of healing and less frustration at the speed of it.
- When you are hurt and hiding, allow interest and joy to lure you out of your retreat. My cat didn't come running when we called, but when we got close, she stood and moved enough for us to carry her to a place where she could be healed.

Sometimes, reclaiming joy isn't a big, uplifting experience. Sometimes, the path toward reclaiming joy is taking painful steps and going through rote actions until we've moved to a place where we can heal better.

Activities

Healing Activity 1
Making Space for Your Feelings

Purpose: To explore what you feel without judgment so later you can make decisions about the feelings.

Sit down with writing tools and think of a time when your feelings were hurt. It can be a fresh hurt that still stings, or you can reach into your past for a hurt that is more comfortably distant. Remember, learning from an old hurt teaches us how to deal with fresher ones. Write down the story of the hurt, the who, what, when, and where of it. Then delve into the why by free writing on the following questions:

- Why do you think this particular situation hurt your feelings?
- Did this hurt connect to other hurts you have and make them worse?
- Would you feel differently if the same situation occurred in a different context or with other people?
- What do you wish you said to the person who hurt you? What would you say right now if there were no consequences?

Feel free to think up your own exploring questions and write the answers to those as well.

These questions are focused on the whys of your feelings, experiences, and reactions without supposing the whys of someone else's behavior.

Repeat this activity for additional hurts, if you wish.

When you are done, put away this writing for several days or a week. After the feelings have settled, see which, if any, still hurt and need an action plan. The next activity will help you create an action plan if you need one.

Healing Activity 2
Taking Action to Heal

Purpose: To create an action plan that helps you begin to heal.

Pick one of your hurts. You might want to start with one of the hurt feelings from Activity 1. On a sheet of paper, write the words: Safety, Trust, and Choices, leaving space to write under each one.

- **Safety.** Decide (and write down) how to create safety for yourself to process this hurt. Safety might look like a solo writing session in a space where you're free to cry. It might look like a night out with a friend who will listen to you rant. It might also look like finding someone with professional expertise (a therapist, coach, or support group) to help you structure your healing.
- **Trust.** Decide and write down how you will create your healing in a way that will not re-traumatize the injury. You need to convince your instinctive brain, the one that wants you to crawl under a bush, that the scary and painful actions you are taking will lead to healing.
- **Choices.** Write down your action plan. It might look like a list of conversations you want to have. It might look like a plan to extricate yourself from an unhealthy situation. What are the choices and actions you will take about your feelings? Now you turn those intended actions into tasks you can start to put on your to do list or calendar.

Healing Activity 3
Interrupting the Shame Spiral

Purpose: To analyze a situation or task where you tend to go into a shame spiral, then make a plan to interrupt that spiral.

Find a task or situation where you tend to end up in a shame spiral. If you can't easily think of one, you can go back to some of the lists you wrote in this book's Finding Center, or Productivity sections to spark your memory of what you might want to tackle.

Following the shame spiral list above, write in the specifics of how your spiral manifests.

Example:

- **Task.** Fold laundry.
- **Failure.** Laundry does not get folded.
- **Shame.** Tell yourself "I'm lazy."
- **Avoid.** Watch an hour of videos on social media.
- **Repeat.** Laundry is still unfolded.

Once you have your spiral written out, make a specific plan for what you will do when you realize you have failed at your task. This action could be an internal re-framing of the failure, giving yourself compassion instead of judgment. It could be a disruption of the shameful thoughts by taking positive actions like going for a walk, eating a meal, or even doing the task.

Pick your action and create a visual reminder of it in a place where you can see it. Try disrupting your shame spirals for a few days or a week, then write and reflect on how that felt.

Note: do not shame spiral if you fail at interrupting your shame spiral. The spirals are strong, and learning to disrupt them is a skill. It will take time and practice to be able to interrupt the spirals.

A Thought Before You Go

In the introduction, I invited you to treat this book like a home tour. At the end of a tour, when your mind is filled with new information, it is good to pause before leaving and decide what to take home with you. We're at that moment with this book. You get to decide what parts of this book get to change your life and what gets left behind when the book closes. Before you leave, however, I'd like to give you one more example of the power of small changes to transform life.

When I moved to my current house, there was a coat closet right by the front door, which was supposed to be useful for storing coats and backpacks. Invariably, the backpacks ended up on the floor and the coats draped over nearby chairs. To enter the house, we had to trip over everything that had not gone inside the closet. Many family meetings were held to correct this issue, but the problem persisted. So, we stepped back and observed to figure out why.

It turned out there were too many steps involved: opening the closet, pulling out the hanger, placing the coat, replacing the hanger in the closet, and closing the door. Also, if the person before you had dropped their things on the floor, the closet door was blocked. It was much easier to drape the coat over a chair in a single motion. Our "misuse" of the entry space was saving time on entry for tired people relieved to be home.

We ripped out the closet and put up coat hooks and cubbies on the wall instead. People could enter, kick the bags and shoes into floor-level cubbies, drop their coats on a hook, and be done. Our entry was much easier to manage because we organized it around how we needed to use the space instead of trying to change the natural habits of the people. We structured our entry to support us instead of the other way around.

> YOUR CREATIVE WORK THRIVES WHEN YOU BUILD THE STRUCTURE THAT WORKS FOR YOU AND THEN READJUST AS NEEDED WHEN YOUR LIFE SHIFTS.

Thank you so much for joining me on this exploration of how to build a life that allows your creativity to flourish. Hopefully, here at the departure point where we say goodbye, you now have new tools and new systems for expanding your capacity for creative work.

I hope my words and activities have been useful to you, but they matter far less than your insights and thoughts. You are the expert in your creative process, a far better expert than I could ever be. Build the system that lets you create. Your process doesn't need to look anything like mine. It only needs to look like yours.

Acknowledgements

Welcome, reader, to this space where I get to spend a moment honoring the support and effort of other people. For you, this section is a list of names of people you don't know, but if you point at one of these names, I can tell you a story of support and love. To tell all those stories in full would require another book's worth of words. Instead, I offer this glimpse into the supporting network of relationships that made this book possible.

I must start with my husband, Howard. When we were dating, he told me that he never wanted to get in the way of me growing. Over the past thirty years, he's done more than that and has actively supported me in my efforts by feeding me (despite dietary restrictions), offering feedback, and making me laugh on the hard days.

Revisionaries is my group of local authors who meet once per month to share food, teach, learn, give feedback, and share in both joys and sorrows. These women have been a stable supporting structure in my life for years now. They are: Hayley Hess-Beaumont, Meg Sherman, Jessica Allred, Daphne Higbee, Heidi Darley, Brittany Wakefield, Nicole Brouwer, Kaitlyn Brouwer, Melissa Muhlenkamp, Mikki Tolley, and Wendy Morkel.

Then there is my Creative Check-In Crew. We meet once per month on Zoom to talk about what is going on in our lives, what creative work we want to get done, and what we've failed to get done. There is a large emphasis on recognizing exactly how many life tasks are part of our creative work. They've listened to me despair and have shared my joy. They are: Kayla Mills, Branson Roskelly, Cordelia Fernwood, Michael Gallowglas, Jess Unrein, Bryan Barnes, and Rebecca Wright.

My smallest group meets weekly on Zoom and is focused on critiquing work for Howard Tayler, Bob Defendi, and myself. Bob went above and beyond for this book, providing editorial feedback for every chapter in rapid-fire fashion when I needed it. I am so grateful he was willing to use his expertise in this way.

My family is not a group that meets on any regular schedule, but my adult children are part of the systems who support me: Keliana Moss, Tyler Moss, Aarik Tayler, Ladmin Tayler, and Aidan Tayler. Thanks also go to my parents, siblings, and siblings-in-law who are always excited when I have news. Sometimes their excitement is what reminds me how cool writing a book is when it feels like hopeless work. A special call out is due to my Grandma Irma Owens, who believed in my writing when I was ten-years-old and paid me a penny per word for anything I wrote.

Another group to whom I owe much is the Writing Excuses Podcasting and Retreat teams. I have learned so much from being around them. Their unwavering belief in my capabilities helped me to believe it as well. Their support during the promotional and marketing parts of this project have carried it further than I could have made it go by myself. They are: Mary Robinette Kowal, DongWon Song, Erin Roberts, Dan Wells, Brandon Sanderson, Emma Reynolds, Marshall Carr, Sarah Sward, Marie Parks, and Jessi Honard.

As a socially anxious person, I'm always a bit astonished when people choose to spend effort to remain in contact with me. That friendship lifts me up, and from that higher perspective I'm able to do more, see more, travel further. Each of these people lifted me up with their friendship: Piper Drake, Matthew Drake, Margaret Dunlap, Kathy Chung, Jennifer Jenkins, Jennifer Jensen, Heather Clark, Janci Patterson, and Emily Sanderson.

Melissa Williams Design did the original art and design for the cover of this book. Traci L. Turner made wonderful graphics I used in my promotional campaigns. A. J. Jepperson provided incredibly insightful editorial feedback. Mykola Bilokonsky let me use his Twitter thread on curiosity-driven motivation as part of one of my chapters.

A much longer list of people are the crowdfunding backers and Patreon supporters. I am grateful to all of them. The Super Supporters are listed here by name:

Allan S
Andrea Hunt
Anne Delekta
Annie McAndrew
Burrow
Cat Gardiner
Christina Goodman
Curtis Frye
David Alex Lamb
David J Owens
David McCabe
David Snell
Devin Aryan
Dodson B. Brown
Don Koch
Elizabeth Galatis
Hans Joachim Seitz
Hunter Wiles
Jacob Johnston
Jeanette Wilde
Jeffrey Naujok
Jen Chu
Jennifer Crispin
Jeremy Budds
John W. Bruce
Jonathan Moore
Kate Montgomery
Kayla Mills
Leane
Linda Monath Gregory
Liz and Justin Braden
Mary Robinette Kowal
Matlatzinca
Matthew Burdett
Maxwell Dunne
Merrick Astronomo
Michael P.
Morrie Mullins
Patrick Brown
Patrick Scott
Peter Foley
Robert Gasper
Ronald Canepa
Rocco Gaskins
Rose Owens
Sarah Ramsey
Stephanie
Steven Joel Zeve
Tillerz
Tyler Mickelson
William Twining
Xander Hacking
Zackary Shumate

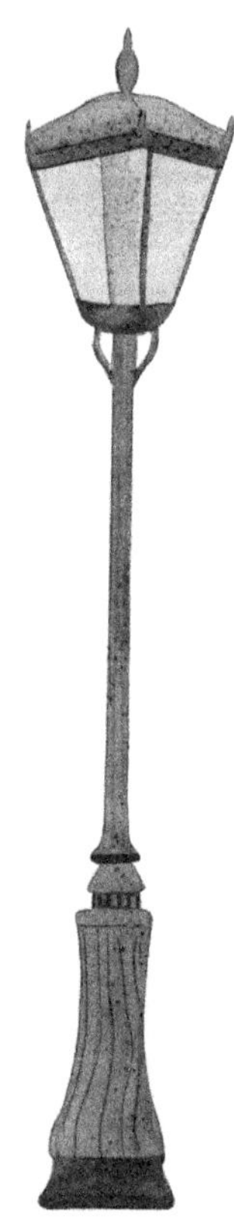

Recommendations

For the reader who wants to dive deeper into some of the topics in this book, I offer a list of books and resources.

- ***A Still Life* by Josie George** – This memoir gives an inside look into the life of a person whose creative work is seriously impacted by disability.
- ***ADHD Alien* by Pina Varnel** (Book coming fall 2026) – These comics do a beautiful job of describing the challenges that ADHD people face and then sometimes providing useful tools for coping with those challenges.
- ***Around the Writer's Block* by Rosane Bane** – This book tackles the neuroscience of avoidance and then provides some tools to help overcome that avoidance.
- ***Being Seen* by Elsa Sjunneson** – Pat memoir, part nonfiction, this book tackles disability from the perspective of a person who is blind.
- ***Burnout: The Secret to Unlocking the Stress Cycle* by Emily Nagoski and Amelia Nagoski** – A deep dive into what causes people to become burned out and then provides some actionable steps toward healing existing burnout and preventing future burnout.
- ***Captainawkward.com* by Jennifer Peepas** – This website is an advice column with deep archives. Reading through these archives taught me a lot about what good relationship boundaries look like and how to set them up in healthy ways.

- ***Gifts of Imperfection* by Brené Brown** – Honestly almost any book by Brené Brown will do. The ways she discusses shame and self compassion are always uplifting.
- **Habitica.com** – This website and app can help you gamifying your tasks in ways that might help you get things done.
- ***How To ADHD* by Jessica McCabe** – This title is both a Book and a YouTube channel. They cover topics related to ADHD from the perspective of a person who has ADHD.
- ***How to Keep House While Drowning* by KC Davis** – An approach to house cleaning when life is overwhelming.
- ***How to Make Stress Your Friend* by Kelly McGonigal** *https://www.ted.com/talks/kelly_mcgonigal_how_to_make_stress_your_friend* – This TED talk helped me re-frame how I thought about stress.
- ***Living with High Functioning Anxiety* by Jordan Raskopoulos** *https://www.ted.com/talks/jordan_raskopoulos_how_i_live_with_high_functioning_anxiety* – This TED talk describes living with High Functioning Anxiety in a way that helped me understand my own anxiety better.
- ***My Grandfather's Blessings* by Rachel Naomi Remen** – A book of short essays from the perspective of someone who counsels people with terminal cancers. Very hopeful and empowering.
- ***Pandemic Productivity* by Jennifer Peepas** *https://captainawkward.com/2020/05/01/pandemic-productivity-life-hacks-from-a-deeply-unproductive-freaked-out-person/* – This article contains some very useful ways to approach getting things done and was part of how I began to use motivational toolboxes other than my familiar ones.
- ***Re-thinking anxiety: Learning to Face Fear* by Dawn Heubner** *https://www.youtube.com/watch?v=jryCoo0BrRk* – This TED talk is full of useful insights into anxiety.
- ***Spoon Theory* by Christine Miserandino** *https://butyoudontlooksick.com/articles/written-by-christine/the-spoon-theory/* – This is the original source for using spoons as a way to describe the challenges of chronic illness.

- **Sweepy** – An app that helps gamify housework in order to help you get it done.
- ***The Four Tendencies* by Gretchen Rubin** – A test and system for helping people diagnose their motivational tendencies.
- ***The Gaslight Effect* by Dr. Robin Stern** – This book fully describes gaslighting behaviors and how you can challenge them.
- ***The Life-Changing Magic of Tidying Up* by Marie Kondo** – The specific methods in this book may be too strict for some people. (They fell apart for Kondo herself once she had three kids) Yet some of the core concepts around how to relate to belongings continue to be helpful even if the specific instructions for managing belongings may not be.
- ***The Moment of Lift* by Melinda Gates** – This book is in large part about the specific work that The Gates Foundation does in advocating for gender equality, however, woven through the book is information about building networks, connecting with others, re-defining existing relationships, and finding balance.
- ***The Not So Big House* by Sarah Susanka and Kira Obolensky** – Some of the information in this book may be dated, but it contains interesting ideas about how to approach our living spaces and make sure they're functioning for the way we actually live.
- ***What My Bones Know* by Stephanie Foo** – A memoir about recovering from complex trauma and c-ptsd.

Sandra Tayler is a writer, editor, and publisher with credits in over thirty different titles. She is a consistently successful crowdfunder, and has spent the last thirty years managing a household alongside several small businesses. Sandra lives in Orem with her husband, three cats, three young adults, and a family of very demanding scrub jays who insist that Sandra's only real job is to put peanuts on the deck rail. You can find Sandra online at sandratayler.com

www.ingramcontent.com/pod-product-compliance
Ingram Content Group UK Ltd.
Pitfield, Milton Keynes, MK11 3LW, UK
UKHW020419250726
13967UKWH00007B/2721